NOBLE VICTORY

A Family's Autism Journey

Mandeep K. Atwal, LL.B.

 FriesenPress

One Printers Way
Altona, MB R0G 0B0
Canada

www.friesenpress.com

ISBN
978-1-03-918680-4 (Hardcover)
978-1-03-918679-8 (Paperback)
978-1-03-918681-1 (eBook)

1. FAMILY & RELATIONSHIPS, AUTISM SPECTRUM DISORDERS

Distributed to the trade by The Ingram Book Company

For all the individuals in the world
living with autism spectrum disorder.

You are seen.

You are heard.

You are respected.

Table of Contents

―――――

Prologue   vii

Chapter 1 - No Room for Error   1

Chapter 2 - Taurus, "the Bull"   9

Chapter 3 - The "Not-So-Typical" Early Years   15

Chapter 4 - Forgive Me, Son   21

Chapter 5 - The Journey Begins   27

Chapter 6 - Light at the End of the Tunnel   39

Chapter 7 - *"Shakti,"* Divine Power   47

Chapter 8 - Power and Strength in Acceptance   55

Chapter 9 - Awareness, Acceptance, Inclusion   69

Chapter 10 - The Struggle is Real   83

Chapter 11 - The "Real World"   89

Chapter 12 - Window of Opportunity   109

Chapter 13 - Help Him, not "Cure" Him   121

Chapter 14 - The Missing Peace   131

Acknowledgements   139

Prologue

OVER THE LAST FIFTEEN YEARS, THE DIAGNOSIS RATE OF autism spectrum disorder in Canada has skyrocketed.[1] There are many theories and medical studies with respect to why this has happened. However, my focus in this book is to look beyond the medical diagnosis of autism and to provide insight into the everyday lives of people living with autism and those who care for and support them through my family's experiences. My hope is that this will create a more complete picture of what autism entails.

On May 12, 2006, my life changed as I became a mother to a beautiful baby boy. Years later, my journey took an unexpected twist when my son was diagnosed with autism spectrum disorder, and motherhood presented even greater challenges for me. My autism journey has made me stronger, more compassionate and empathetic toward other people, and a fierce advocate for those who face judgmental attitudes and a loss of opportunities simply because of a diagnosis. These individuals shouldn't be defined by their diagnosis. They are so much more than a diagnosis, and I believe it's my duty in this life to bring to light the gifts that these individuals can provide to this world—gifts this world so desperately needs.

My main motivation for writing this book is to help people who are facing challenges similar to my own. Helping other families who are struggling through different challenges and obstacles in their autism journeys is my passion. Although my book may not solve everyone's challenges, I pray

---

1 "Infographic: Autism Spectrum Disorder among Children and Youth in Canada," Government of Canada, last modified March 29, 2018, https://www.canada.ca/en/public-health/services/publications/diseases-conditions/infographic-autism-spectrum-disorder-children-youth-canada-2018.html.

that it provides you with strength, power, confidence, inspiration, acceptance, inclusion, resilience, faith, and most importantly, hope. Moreover, I hope that those who want to learn a little more about autism, specifically through one family's challenges, find my book to be a very honest and practical look at how emotionally and physically challenging it can be to raise a child on the spectrum. The name of my book comes from two of the most powerful and driving forces in my life—my son, JSS, whose name means "Guardian of Victory," and my daughter, AKS, whose name means "Noble Woman."

I want to dedicate this book to all the individuals who are living with autism. Many people in society may not see you as a guiding force in the world, but I do. I have learned that autism gives you the special ability to bring an innocence, an open-mindedness, and a unique perspective to a world that can at times be very closed-minded and judgmental. This is a very powerful gift, and there is a reason God gave you this gift. People living with autism continue to be judged on the basis of their diagnosis alone and often fall victim to preconceived notions that some people have about those living with autism.

My son has also faced these challenges. Although this has been very disheartening and frustrating, it only illustrates to us how much more work needs to be done. It also fuels the fire in our souls and strengthens our resolve to raise awareness and educate people about autism. I hope that through our advocacy for autism, we can show others that those living with autism may be "different, not less" (as Dr. Temple Grandin has said many times). Awareness is the first step, but inclusion is the necessary second step. We will never give up. Thank you for trusting us to be your mothers, fathers, siblings, grandparents, teachers, aides, guardians, and friends. I hope we have given you the care, nurturing, and support that you deserve. You have all changed my life and helped my soul to grow. We have learned so much from you and continue to do so. We will always stand by you and support you in making this world a more educated and inclusive place. God bless you, and may all your dreams come true.

"Injustice anywhere is a threat to justice everywhere."

Dr. Martin Luther King Jr.

CHAPTER 1
No Room for Error

The Plan

"Everything must go according to the plan;
No room for error,
No exceptions to the rule.
A destination awaits me on a path unknown,
My soul journey guides me as I forge ahead.
Determination and hard work are the key,
To create a perfect life for me."

Mandeep K. Atwal
September 8, 2021

BY THE AGE OF SEVEN, I HAD EVERYTHING PLANNED—WHAT was going to happen in my life, what I was going to do to succeed, and how I was going to accomplish all of my goals. I knew I wanted to be a lawyer, and this became a passionate dream of mine. This was a big dream for such a little child, and I'm sure the challenges I faced growing up in one of the only South Asian families in a small city in Alberta contributed to this dream. Facing discrimination and racism, as well as being afraid to show the world who I really was out of a fear of being alienated, definitely contributed to my desire to become a lawyer. I also believe that I faced such challenging situations in order to prepare me for my soul journey. Only by going through these experiences was I able to conclude that I wanted to stand up for what I believed was right. My soul was shaping the direction of my life from a very young age.

As a child, when I would face discrimination or racism and be excluded, I couldn't understand why I was treated differently. I had a lot of questions for my parents, and I was shocked and confused when I heard their answer; I didn't understand how anyone could think that the colour of my skin made me any less of a person. I wanted to come up with a solution, so I announced that I would become a lawyer and change the world. Justice and equality for all people mattered to me.

As I grew up, I got involved with organizations that gave me the opportunity to deliver speeches on many different social justice issues including equality based on race, gender, and disability. I joined various public speaking platforms to develop my skills. I embraced any opportunity that came my way that would help me fine-tune my advocacy and critical thinking skills and provide me with the opportunity to increase my comfort level while speaking in public. I pursued many avenues to feed the passion in my heart. I joined speech and debate clubs, I participated in local and provincial rotary music festivals, I became a part of peer support clubs, I entered many public speaking competitions, I spoke at school assemblies, I was the master of ceremonies at my high school graduation, and I appeared in our local newspaper and a local talk show for my involvement in various community events. All these experiences made me feel like I was heading in the right direction in my life.

I even had the opportunity to visit the United Nations after winning the grand prize at a public speaking competition. At the age of sixteen, I toured parts of Canada and the United States for three weeks with a group of students from British Columbia, Alberta, and Saskatchewan, all of whom had also won an equivalent public speaking competition. I also had the opportunity to sit on a panel as the student delegate with a well-known Canadian journalist and members of the community and debate the issue of media censorship. I felt like an old soul in a young body. I took life pretty seriously; I definitely wasn't a free spirit.

I recall an article that I wrote—published in our local newspaper—that encompassed the essence of my belief system. Ironically, one Canada Day, I was out with my family to watch the fireworks, and I heard a middle-aged man making some extremely racist remarks. They weren't directed at a particular person, but rather toward an entire ethnic group. I was stunned at the level of ignorance and racism I was witnessing. It brought me back to the days of being a child, bullied for the colour of my skin. Instead of approaching the man and telling him off, I decided to submit an article to our local paper expressing what I had seen in the hopes of reaching a greater audience and raising awareness about the mindset of some people in our community. Something in my soul gave me the confidence and strength to advocate for equality and thus challenge narrow-minded belief systems. We all have a voice, but due to circumstances beyond our control, not everyone is able to use theirs. I wanted to stand up and speak for those who had something very important to say but weren't afforded the same opportunities I had been.

A speech I prepared for an original oratory competition reverberates in my mind to this day. I was fifteen years old, and I stood before a panel of judges in a small town in Northern Alberta to speak about the tremendous strength of character and power of one man who, during extremely turbulent times, was strong enough to stand up for a community who had faced, and continues to face, systemic discrimination—Dr. Martin Luther King Jr. His famous quote "Injustice anywhere is a threat to justice everywhere" resonated with my soul, and I still carry those words with me today as a mantra to give me the strength to face and fight against injustice. Even though it was quite apparent that the judging panel wasn't impressed or receptive to my speech, I didn't care. There was a fire in me that was growing stronger, and I didn't realize then how that would play a critical role in my life.

Strengthening my advocacy skills wasn't the only thing that fed the fire in my soul. At the age of twelve, my mom enrolled me in Tae Kwon Do. She wanted me to be independent, educated, and strong both emotionally and physically. My mom had a traditional upbringing and immigrated to Canada from India in the early 1970s. She saw the fire in my soul, and as any good mother would, she lifted me up, making me stronger. She wanted to ensure that I had all the opportunities her own life circumstances hadn't allowed her to pursue. I was scared when I first started Tae Kwon Do and had to spar other kids, but I quickly realized that physical and mental strength were closely tied together. At the age of seventeen, I received my black belt in Tae Kwon Do. Reaching this milestone had increased my mental strength, which in turn gave me a greater sense of self-confidence— I knew I could advocate for myself verbally and defend myself physically. I felt my spiritual energy, strength, and power growing.

Although I was confident in my ability to stand up for myself, I still wanted to do more. I wanted to do something important in my life, not just for me, but for others. Higher education was an important piece of this puzzle for me. Throughout my childhood and my high school years, I worked very hard and studied a lot. My dream was to move to Toronto, Ontario and become a criminal lawyer in a large criminal law firm. It was a big dream, but I had an undying determination that I now understand as my soul pushing me to fulfill my soul journey. Nothing was easy, but all the time and effort that I put into my studies paid off as I made the honour roll throughout high school and received many academic accolades. After graduating from grade 12, my plan was to earn my bachelor of arts degree in political science from the University of Calgary, and then head off to law school—and that was exactly what I did. I attended the University of Ottawa Law School. Everything was going according to my plan. I had the education, confidence, family support, and faith in God to continue on my path. There was no room for error.

Even with my soul pushing me to become a lawyer and a tenacious advocate, I also knew that one day, I wanted to be a mother; this was very important to me. I loved children, and I knew I wanted to stay at home with my children and not work outside of the home until they were in school full-time. My mom had stayed home with us, and I had a tremendous amount of respect for her, so I wanted to give my children the same upbringing, foundation, and loving home I had known growing up. Needless to say, this seemed far off in the distant future; I knew that marriage and children would happen only after I was called to the Ontario Bar and became a full-fledged lawyer.

After saying my tearful goodbyes to my family in September 1995, I headed off to Ottawa, Ontario to continue fulfilling my dreams. There were many days I felt scared and alone being so far from home, and I questioned my decision and my ability to accomplish all the things I wanted to, but my faith played a huge role in my life. I knew that I was being taken care of and that there was a reason I was two thousand miles away from home. Despite getting very sick in my first year of law school, I managed to push myself forward and ended up graduating with my class on time. The fire in my soul wouldn't let me slow down. Even my doctor said he had never seen a recovery as quick in anyone who was suffering from the same ailment.

I continued to forge ahead; however, I would be remiss to say that I never doubted myself, faced difficult obstacles and challenges, or became afraid of failing. Growing up, everyone faces situations where others try to push them down or make their life more difficult than it needs to be merely out of jealousy or insecurity. I don't want to spend my time focusing on these situations because I feel the important lesson for me is what I learned from them and how I increased my determination and resiliency in the face of extreme negativity. In the spring of 1998, I graduated from law school, and in June 1998, I moved to Toronto, Ontario. I was exactly where I dreamt of being and doing exactly what I dreamt of doing. I began working with the then-largest criminal law firm in Canada. The goals and dreams I had set for myself were coming to fruition in exactly the way I had imagined.

Working with the criminal law firm was exciting and challenging at the same time. Criminal defence work isn't easy. One can become very jaded, depressed, pessimistic, and disillusioned in this type of environment. It's easy to lose sight of why you're doing the work you're doing. I witnessed a lot of unjust acts being committed against accused persons. I saw how drugs and alcohol can destroy a person's life. I witnessed unfair life circumstances, including poverty, abusive home environments, and a complete lack of support for people with special needs. These scenarios became all too common during my time working as a criminal defence lawyer. I often felt I didn't even have time to breathe due to the intensity of the workload, the demands of the job, and the mental fatigue I would feel at the end of the day. There was no time to engage in self or circumstantial reflection. I was running around like a chicken with my head cut off, so I filed these experiences away in my mind. Only when I became a mother did I find them creeping back into my mind for further reflection.

Still, my life plan continued on its designated track. I met my future husband, Samir, at work. We worked at the same law firm, and we bonded over similar experiences, frustrations, and challenges while working in a criminal law environment. We became friends, as we both had the same passion to fight against injustice, stand up for the underdog, and ensure equality for everyone the best we could. We carried the same moral compass and had the same value system. We had a soul connection, and only later would I come to realize why our souls were brought together in this lifetime. After being friends for over a year, we started dating, got engaged, and were married on July 27, 2002.

As I continued to work as a criminal defence lawyer, I realized something was missing in my life, but I couldn't put my finger on it. Wasn't I exactly where I wanted to be? Why had I worked so hard to get here, only to feel confused and disillusioned? I realized I couldn't see myself practicing criminal law for the rest of my life. I went on to practice immigration law for a period of time, but I still felt like something was missing and I wasn't where I was supposed to be or doing what my soul was supposed to do on earth. I knew I had a special calling in life; however, I felt like I was losing sight of what that might have been. I'd never felt this way before. Even amid this confusion, there was still an ongoing determination and continuous fire and strength in my soul that kept me going. I wasn't sure what the fire was burning for, but I knew that giving up wasn't an option.

I had a plan, and everything had gone according to that plan, but I knew that even though I could be successful practicing criminal or immigration law, it just wasn't where I wanted to be. With all the questions and uncertainty looming in my mind, I started to feel like maybe it was time to start a family. Perhaps once that step in my plan was completed, I would find more balance and peace—maybe that was the missing piece. Eventually, Samir and I decided to move back to Alberta to be closer to my family and start our own. I was very close to my mom and knew I would need her support, and besides, Calgary seemed like a good city to raise a family.

In June 2005, Samir and I moved to Calgary, Alberta and started our new life. I was thankful that Samir found a job before our move, as my plan was to be at home with my children for a maximum of five or six years before returning to the workforce and fueling the passion I had in my soul to do something great and make a difference in this world. I just wasn't sure how I would do it or even what it was that I was seeking; I just knew that standing up for others had something to do with it. Unbeknownst to me, the passion to do something great and to fight for justice would not be found in the workplace, but instead right in my own home.

CHAPTER 2
Taurus, "the Bull"

———

A Gift from God

"I loved you before I met you.
You were a guiding light in my life even before I had you.
When I held you in my arms for the first time,
I didn't know the lessons that I would learn from you.

You have been my soul teacher.
You have been my inspiration.
You have been my resiliency.

The greatest joy in my life is to watch you succeed.
My soul resonates with pride and strength.
You raise my vibration.

I am blessed and honoured to call you my son."

Mandeep K. Atwal
May 7, 2018

THERE WERE MULTIPLE COMPLICATIONS DURING MY DELIV-
ery of JSS. It was a long and painful process. JSS was born approximately
thirty-three hours after my water had "broken." After being sent home
twice due to the maternity ward being at capacity, my labour was finally
induced. It was as if everything that could go wrong did go wrong. I didn't

receive an epidural until eleven hours after I was induced, as my labour was progressing very slowly. The first attempt at administering my epidural didn't work, so the needle was reinserted a second time.

In the meantime, I received a variety of pain medications in an attempt to alleviate my extreme discomfort. I wasn't used to taking so much medication, and the entire process was taking a toll on my body. Things finally came to a head after I had been pushing for hours; the doctors came into the room and told me that I had a fever and that my baby's heart rate was very high. The baby had to be delivered in the next fifteen minutes or I would have to have an emergency caesarean section. We were asked whether we wanted to use the vacuum extractor or forceps for the delivery. We elected for the forceps, and I was told that I would have to give one big push in order to deliver the baby. I was scared but determined. The doctor said to me, "On the count of three, I need you to give me one big push." I listened intently to the count. "One, two, three." When I heard the word "push," I gave it all the power and strength that was left in my body. The next thing I heard was, "It's a boy!" My heart was filled with love and joy for a split second, and then I remember thinking, "I'm tired. I just want to close my eyes for a moment." What happened to me next was something I had read and heard about but never expected to experience. I wasn't sure whether I was going to put this experience in my book, as it's very personal, intense, and life-changing; however, upon reflection, I decided that it's part of my story, and it definitely played a role in shaping me into the person I am today.

When I closed my eyes, I saw many images flashing before me. It was like the movie of my life was playing at an extremely high speed. I seem to remember it being played backward, from that day in the hospital to the day I was born, or perhaps it was a film of all of my past lives—I couldn't be sure. This film strip played in a flash, and the next thing I knew, I saw a huge white light. It encompassed the entire space around me. I knew I was there, but I wasn't in my physical form. I was energy.

I remember pleading for my life with the white light. My communication, however, wasn't occurring through words. It was through my thoughts and my mind—in other words, telepathically. I knew that whoever was there was listening to and understanding every word that I was saying, even though I never received any type of response. The first

A Family's Autism Journey

thing I communicated was that my parents wouldn't be able to go on if I died. I urged the light to understand that my siblings and friends would be able to go on if I wasn't there, but I knew my parents wouldn't be able to handle the loss of their child. I then said that I didn't even get a chance to see my parents hold their first grandchild or watch my husband and sisters hold my baby boy. The final thing I said was that I never even got the opportunity to see my son's face or hold my baby. I was begging for my life—to go back to all the people who loved me. I was so desperate to come back.

The next thing I knew, I was opening my eyes, and everything was white. There was an oxygen mask over my face and what felt like fifteen doctors and nurses surrounding me. I recall asking the doctor, "Where am I—am I in heaven?" and "Am I going to die?" She answered the first question but not the second. There were wires and tubes everywhere; I had intravenous fluid lines in my foot and one in my arm. I couldn't see my baby, Samir, Mom, or my best friend, Maira, anywhere. They had all been taking turns supporting me through the delivery, but now, I didn't see them around. I remember thinking, "What is happening?" I knew something had gone wrong.

Slowly, the doctors and nurses moved away from me, and I could see my little boy in a little bed with a heat lamp on him. He looked completely relaxed, and I remember saying, "Thank you, God." It was later that I realized that God wasn't behind the light; He was, in fact, "the light," and what I had experienced was a near-death experience. I found out afterward that I'd had a major haemorrhage, and my blood pressure had dropped to forty over twenty-one. I was lucky to be alive.

My little Taurus "the bull" baby was born on May 12, 2006, at 12:55 p.m., two weeks before his due date. I loved reading about horoscopes, and I knew my Taurus baby would be stubborn but loyal. I felt like I had been waiting for him my entire life. I decided to give him the name my mom had chosen for me if I was a boy. The meaning of JSS's name is "Guardian of Victory." I loved the name, and at the time, I didn't think about the depth the meaning of his name would carry. As the years would progress, I would come to realize this was absolutely the perfect name for my baby boy.

11

After things had calmed down in my hospital room, I found out that JSS was born with the cord around his neck, and they had asked Samir whether they should cut the cord or try and remove it by lifting it over his head. The doctors made this inquiry because we wanted to store JSS's stem cells, and if the cord was cut, this would drastically reduce the number of useable stem cells. Samir made the right decision by telling them to cut the cord immediately. He didn't want to jeopardize JSS's oxygen supply. In 2006, from our experience, not many people were storing stem cells. None of our friends had stored their child's stem cells, but it was something that came to me with an overpowering force one day when I was about five months pregnant and saw a commercial for the storage of stem cells. I just knew it had to be done, and it was very important to me. Only a decade later would I discover why.

◆ ◆ ◆

As a new mother, I faced a lot of challenges, just as many mothers do. I was in the hospital for five days after the delivery, as I had lost a lot of blood. Due to the trauma of the delivery, JSS was slow to feed, and my body was still recovering. The forceps delivery caused JSS to have a headache for a day or so, and he also had a little jaundice. I kept thinking, "This is all temporary, and things are going to get better." We both had been through the wringer, but every mother faced these challenges. Before we were discharged, we were also told that there was a slight murmur in JSS's heart, and it would have to be checked out in two months' time to ensure it wasn't anything serious. I patiently listened to everything, but I was itching to get out of the hospital. It had been a long nine months of sickness and bed rest, followed by a tough delivery, and I was ready to go home.

Naïvely, I thought being at home was going to make everything better, but the problems of motherhood were only beginning. I was still in a tremendous amount of pain, and I was having trouble walking, but I was so thankful for my mom throughout these early months. Without her, I wouldn't have made it.

The first year of JSS's life was tough. I knew that babies cried and didn't necessarily have a sleep schedule, but JSS definitely marched to the beat of his own drum. He wasn't a good sleeper and woke up every forty-five minutes at night. In addition to him not sleeping well, he also didn't eat well. He was having a lot of stomach pains, so feedings were very difficult. We tried many different formulas, and finally, when he was three months old, we took him for a blood test to see if he had a milk allergy. It was a relief to find out that he didn't have a milk allergy; however, the challenges with feedings continued and we couldn't understand why.

JSS also had terrible eczema, and we made numerous dermatologist visits in an attempt to figure out how we could best help him. We spent hours at bath time making sure we followed all of the things the doctor had told us about what creams to apply and how to keep his eczema from flaring up. When JSS was about two months old, he started getting cradle cap, and it progressed to the point where he lost all his hair. It was around this time that we also followed up with the cardiologist with respect to JSS's heart murmur. We were relieved to learn that the small hole in his heart had closed up and that he didn't have a heart problem.

In the first fifteen months of life, JSS had six ear infections, which included tremendous ear pain, very high fevers, and numerous hospital and doctors' visits. He was treated with antibiotics for each ear infection. I felt completely overwhelmed. I didn't feel like we were really living; rather, we were just surviving. As time moved along, I kept reassuring myself that things would get better, and in time, we would have a "normal" life. At the time, I had no idea that this was only the beginning of an extraordinary journey.

CHAPTER 3
The "Not-So-Typical" Early Years

Acceptance

"To live, one must accept:
Accept the fate one has been handed;
Accept the life one has been given.

Denial is pain;
Acceptance is peace;

A peace that gets one through the days and nights;
A peace that gets one through the struggles and the triumphs;

Accepting one's cross is not an easy thing to do.
But the strength that one gets from carrying this burden will
follow her her whole life through.

Burden translates into strength,
Strength translates into accomplishment,
And accomplishment translates into peace."

Mandeep K. Atwal
September 8, 2005

I FELT AS THOUGH I DIDN'T GET TO ENJOY THE FIRST YEAR OF
my child's life like other mothers. While other mothers were having playdates with their kids and socializing, I was dragging myself, one sleepless

night after another, to physiotherapy with severe sciatic issues that occurred during the delivery. My recovery was long and hard. Although I tried to be realistic—I knew it wasn't all fun and games for other mothers—I still felt as though my struggle had taken a toll on me. I was sad. Most days, I was barely surviving as I put JSS in a stroller and walked for hours so he would sleep. While we had moved closer to her, my mom still didn't live in the same city, and I was often alone all day caring for JSS. Friendships seemed to fall by the wayside as I spent all my time and energy caring for JSS.

When I was eight months pregnant, I had a dream where my maternal grandfather, Papa ji, came to me and said I should put a white rosary, which had been given to him, in JSS's room. I didn't even know such a rosary existed until I called my mom and she told me she had the rosary. Needless to say, I put the rosary in JSS's room before he was born, and it's been there since that day. Sometimes late at night, I would hold the rosary and ask my grandfather to help me and make things better. I knew he was watching over JSS as his guardian angel.

As time moved along, JSS hit his milestones like a typically developing child, and I was relieved with this progression. He sat up at six months, crawled at about eight months, said his first word at ten months, started walking at thirteen months, responded to his name early on, played with toys, laughed, and loved cuddles. However, he had a hard time with different textures of foods, and he would choke if his food wasn't cut into small pieces. We had to feed him every meal, but I didn't see this as a big problem.

We had a big birthday party for JSS for his first birthday in a banquet hall. This was typical for a South Asian family. JSS was the first grandchild on both sides of the family, and his first birthday was a huge day to celebrate. That night, he cried for almost the entire party until he finally fell asleep. People told me that some kids don't like a lot of noise and that perhaps he was overtired, but that this was all normal. I was also not too concerned at this time, as I could understand why a child could find this type of environment overstimulating.

However, we noticed that whenever we took JSS out to the mall, someone's house, or any public place, he would spend most of his time crying and upset. We couldn't figure out why. We watched as other kids played, grabbed finger foods, and ate while I would be sitting on a couch with JSS crying in my lap. I would be rocking him and trying to feed him the pureed food that I had brought along. I had no idea why he was so upset. Why wasn't he behaving like all the other children? What was bothering him? Why were we experiencing the "typical years" in such a "nontypical" way?

When JSS was eighteen months old, we noticed that his speech wasn't progressing. He said his first word when he was ten months old, but he hadn't acquired much more language since then. When I talked to other mothers and people in the community, I was often reassured that some children, especially boys, speak later and that this wasn't a cause for concern. I was mostly relieved when I heard this; however, in my heart, I was concerned.

Whenever we went out anywhere, I was always watching the other children to see how their behaviour compared to my son's. I would casually ask all the mothers about their experiences with their kids and then in my mind analyze how JSS's behaviour compared. My brain was always "on," trying to figure out if something was wrong, if there was something I should be worried about. One of the things I noticed was that between the ages of eighteen months and two years, JSS's crying in social settings was hit and miss, but the one thing that was constant was his extreme energy. I'm not talking about the typical amount of energy a toddler has, where parents find themselves exhausted at the end of the day. I'm talking about an intense energy, as if he was driven by a motor.

If we went to anyone's house, I couldn't sit for even one minute. I would be chasing JSS as he jumped around and ran, flapped his arms in excitement, opened and closed doors many, many times, grabbed everything and anything on the counters, grabbed kids and hugged them, and went into every room to check everything out. As I was sweating and running around after JSS making sure he didn't destroy the house or hurt himself by accident, I often thought the other mothers must be staring at me with astonishment as they sipped their coffees and watched their kids playing. It didn't help that JSS held his own in the weight category. Carrying and lifting him took a serious toll on my body and seemed to set me back with respect to any progress I made in healing my sciatica problems. After an hour or so of chasing JSS, trying to drink a coffee while climbing up and down stairs, and engaging in what seemed to be a never-ending obstacle course, I would be done. I would tell the other mothers it was time for me to go, and I would frantically try and catch JSS and get him into the car so I could take a breath. Once he was strapped in the car seat, I would breathe a sigh of relief and head home completely exhausted.

Not surprisingly, I stopped going to people's houses, and they stopped inviting me. I felt alone and sad, as if no one could understand my situation or how I was feeling. How could they possibly understand when even I didn't know what was happening? So, life went on. I was still pretty sleep-deprived, as JSS continued waking up many times during the night and then was up for the day at 5 a.m. I was physically and mentally exhausted from all of JSS's energy. It was difficult without a break—Samir worked all day, and I didn't have any family close by to help me. I didn't dream of leaving JSS with a babysitter, as I was always worried about how he would communicate his needs. The only audible word he had was "Mama." I woke up each day praying that God would grant me the strength to get through another day. I had to become creative so I could sit for a few minutes a day. I put gates up everywhere and blocked off so many areas in our house that even leaving our family room became a series of hurdles and acrobatics that would seriously test my flexibility.

I would sit most days and think, "Is this my life? Are things ever going to get better? Did I spend nine years of post-secondary education and training to become a lawyer only to be sitting in a caged-up family room? Is my life resigned to running to doctors' offices to deal with high fevers, ear infections, and eczema? I'm not a teacher; aren't kids supposed to just learn to speak by listening to us?" I admit, I felt sorry for myself, and I didn't know anyone who was going through the same thing as me.

In June 2008, after JSS had just turned two years old, we were invited to a birthday party in my friend's home. I was hesitant to go, especially since it was a midday party and Samir was working and would be unable to attend and help me. Ordinarily, when we went to social events, Samir and I would trade off taking care of JSS so we could each have the opportunity to socialize and quickly eat. However, I was pretty lonely, and I hadn't met my friends in a while, so I decided to bite the bullet and go to the party alone. Whatever was meant to be would happen.

I also felt bad whenever I denied JSS the opportunities to go to these events, as he was very social and loved meeting other kids, although his intense hugs often took kids by surprise. Respecting social boundaries was definitely not a course I pictured JSS teaching in the future. As a mother, I could see that my little boy was very loving and that he just wanted to have fun like other kids. Many days, I was torn. I would question whether I was doing what was best for him, whether he was getting what he needed, whether he needed more friends. The one thing I did know was that I loved him more than anything in the world, and I was very protective of him. I always tried to make sure I met his needs in the best way possible.

So we headed off to the birthday party. I took a deep breath before we left the car, and I prayed that JSS would be a little less wild today. It actually turned out to be a good day, one that would change the course of my life. JSS didn't cry as much as usual on this day, as he became very busy with the Thomas the Tank Engine trains and train table. He would line up the trains, flap his arms, rock his body back and forth, and mumble sounds as he played with the trains. I sat down and watched him and the other children play. I listened as other children of the same age chatted away. To my surprise, some kids even spoke in four- and five-word sentences! I always found myself analyzing the behaviour of other kids in an attempt to figure out if JSS's behaviour and language development was on track.

As we were getting ready to leave, one of the other moms at the party had a little girl who was the same age as JSS. The little girl was chatting away, and I started talking to her mom, who happened to be a speech language pathologist. I told her that her daughter's language was so advanced and that perhaps little girls were more advanced in speech than boys. Then I asked her a question and received an answer I wasn't prepared for at all.

I told her about JSS's language development, or lack thereof, and how he had a hard time understanding multistep instructions. I asked her if I should be worried or if things would work themselves out. She firmly told me, "I would be worried." Her words hit me like a ton of bricks. I was stunned and felt as if someone had pierced my heart with a spear. I was thankful for her honest response, but there isn't a loving mother on this earth who wants to hear that there may be something "wrong" with her child. Everything around me seemed hazy and muffled as I tried listening to her explain where and how I could find help. I was physically present, but my mind was somewhere else; it was as if I was having an out-of-body experience. Somehow, I got myself together, and JSS and I left the party.

My mind was racing all the way home. All my questions were overlapping one another. How worried should I be? Is this a speech delay or something more? Would he catch up to other kids his age? Was I making a big deal out of nothing? What would his future look like? I arrived at home and got JSS settled in where I could keep a close eye on him. I picked up the phone and called Alberta Health Services, and I told them I needed to book an appointment with a speech language pathologist to help my son. I knew it was the right thing to do, but it also felt like an admission that something was wrong. Making the call was easy—I would do anything for my son—but the realization that JSS was facing a developmental challenge was becoming a reality I wasn't ready to accept.

CHAPTER 4
Forgive Me, Son

Forgive Me, Son

"Forgive me, dear son, if I am hard on you.
I am trying to get you ready for life so no one can hurt you.

I fear that I will not be here every day,
To make your pain and suffering go away.

So I push you hard in school and life
So you can succeed and shine bright.

I fear the world and how it will treat you
When I can't be there to protect you.

Forgive me, son, I never want to hurt you.
The reason I am tough is to make you the best person you can be.

Forgive me, son, for I love you so that the thought of you in pain
or sad kills my soul."

Mandeep K. Atwal
November 4, 2020

IN NOVEMBER 2008, JSS BEGAN SPEECH THERAPY WITH A speech language pathologist. Samir and I would both attend the sessions. I had given up a lot in the last two years with respect to my personal life, but another thing that I had to give up, which was very difficult for me, was teaching JSS our mother tongue. I was fluent in Punjabi, and I had been speaking Punjabi with JSS since he was born. It was very important to me to retain this aspect of our culture. However, over time, I realized that with JSS's limited vocabulary, which essentially consisted of sounds, Samir and I had to accept the fact that it was time for me to start speaking to JSS in English only. It would be very difficult for him to grasp two languages, as he was already having such a difficult time communicating, and if he could only speak one language, it had to be English. So with a heavy heart, I started to speak to JSS in only English.

Samir and I were the only ones who understood JSS's language and his needs. We were very in tune with JSS and understood him by listening to his heart and soul, not just his limited words and sounds. The days were long and hard, and the stress and worry that Samir and I had about JSS's life and future was the only thing we could really focus on.

I remember one day standing in front of the pantry door with JSS crying and pushing me. I knew he wanted a cookie, and I could just give it to him, but I wanted my son to take steps, albeit small ones, so he could progress in life. He had to go to school and meet people, and I was concerned he wouldn't be able to communicate his needs, so I focused on helping him to try and express himself. Day after day, I pushed him to succeed. I would stand at the pantry door and look at him and say, "Cookie, cookie." After a lot of crying and screaming, he would finally push the sound out: "cooo." Good enough for me. He tried, and he got the cookie. I remember walking over to the couch, watching JSS eat his cookie, which I had to cut up into little pieces so he wouldn't choke, and then sitting down and crying. "Forgive me, son, for pushing you so hard," I thought to myself.

I was mentally exhausted. I was scared. I wondered what path life was taking us on. I never loved anyone the way I loved JSS, and to see him struggle tore up my heart and soul. He was teaching me the true meaning of unconditional love, and I also learned that loving unconditionally can cause a pain in your heart like no other. Words couldn't express my heart-ache and fear.

As I looked at my son's beautiful brown eyes and cute little face, I wished I could make his life perfect. I wished I could take his pain away. I wanted to make his pain and frustration a burden I would carry for him. But that wasn't to be, and I felt helpless. The only thing I knew I could successfully do for him was to pursue every avenue of therapy and support for him so he could continue to progress and grow. I felt sad, but I never ever lost hope, and I knew I would never give up. The fire in my soul was still there; however, my soul was also filled with more heartache and pain.

Life moved on, and every day from 6:30 a.m. to 10:30 p.m., when JSS would finally fall asleep, I persevered. JSS's energy level was out of this world, and I found it very difficult to keep up with him, especially when I took him out alone. Managing a child who couldn't speak, who was unable to express his needs, and was unable to understand what I was saying to him felt like an insurmountable challenge. I couldn't even dream of having guests over to our home, as it would be impossible for me to entertain alone and keep an eye on JSS. This was something that not everyone understood.

Furthermore, at every opportunity, as soon as JSS saw another child, he would grab the child and hug them. It went without saying that not many children liked this. JSS loved kids, and he loved being around people; he just had a unique way of socializing. All of these obstacles forced me to find innovative ways to teach him. I showed him a lot of pictures in books; I would show him different items in the house and repeat over and over what they were and how they worked; we would watch kids' television shows and I would say to him, when kids were playing together on the show, "No hug, play."

I would go to the store and buy different food items like pineapples, avocados, and kiwis in an attempt to increase his vocabulary and give him the opportunity to feel the texture of the food and smell the item. I would explain to him that it was food and then demonstrate to him what to do with it by pretending to eat the food. JSS used his senses in a different way than most people, and I needed to find a way to teach him that benefitted him. Looking at pictures in books wasn't enough. He needed to experience everything, and this gave him more understanding and context.

I was amazed at how other children just heard a word once and remembered it while also knowing the context in which that word should be used. I was also surprised at how other kids would listen to their parents, and even if they couldn't communicate fully yet, they knew exactly what their parents were asking them to do. I couldn't understand why JSS was having such a hard time with simple language and instructions. Was it because he was so hyperactive that his brain didn't calm down enough to allow for processing time? Was it just a matter of time before things got better and he just needed that "aha" moment? Was I doing something wrong? I didn't know the answers to any of these questions. What I did know was that after repeating words and phrases over and over again, day after day, I had no idea if I was getting anywhere or what our future held for us, and I was completely drained.

I recall one day where I just felt completely overwhelmed. I couldn't take it anymore. I walked into our dining room where JSS wouldn't be able to see me, and I curled up in a little ball and quietly sobbed. I felt broken, destroyed, confused, and tired. I wanted all this to stop. I wanted a different life. As I quietly broke down, I felt a little hand on my shoulder. It was the softest, gentlest touch. I looked up, and as tears streamed down my face, I saw the face of my beautiful little boy. His big brown eyes were staring down at me, and he had an inquisitive look in his eyes. He wasn't able to speak, but his eyes told me exactly what he wanted to say. He put his hand in front of him and made a questioning gesture that said to me, "Mom, what's wrong? What's going on?" It took me less than a second to grab that little boy and hug and kiss him harder than I ever had before. He giggled as I held him in my arms. I loved him so much. There wasn't anything I wouldn't or couldn't do for him. I would go to the ends of the earth to make sure that he was happy and that he had everything he needed.

After that moment of weakness, I suddenly felt a little stronger. That strength was like a drop in a bucket; it didn't seem like much, but it was a drop that wasn't there the day before. As I look back now, I realize the strength I felt on that day stemmed from the unconditional love that I had for my son. He had given me a true gift. He had taught me that even during times of tremendous desperation, love can give you strength.

In March 2009, we headed off to speech therapy. It was our last visit, as the program was coming to an end, and it was also a day that changed my life. JSS was two months away from his third birthday, and he still only had a vocabulary of sounds. The only word he clearly said was "Mama." We walked into the therapy room, and the therapist began her play therapy with JSS. JSS happily played with her, but he would only make sounds or flap his arms when he was very excited. The speech therapist tried many times to get JSS to say hello while they played with little animals on a farm set. "Hello, hello," she repeated over and over again. I was praying, hoping, and begging God to have JSS say hello back to her.

Finally, after numerous attempts by the speech language pathologist, JSS said, "Hhhiii."

"This is it," I thought, "He's going to be okay! He's listening and following instructions. It just takes him a little longer than other kids."

"Good boy! Yes, hi!" I exclaimed.

This excitement was short-lived. JSS continued to play with the toys, and the speech language pathologist sat down to speak with me and Samir. She told us that this was the last session, and that JSS would continue to need therapy. I thought to myself, "This isn't a problem; I would take him wherever he needed to go." I knew he still needed speech therapy, as he was almost three years old and wasn't speaking yet.

She continued, telling us that JSS would benefit from the support of a multidisciplinary team, which would include a speech language pathologist, an occupational therapist, a behavioural therapist, a physiotherapist—to work on gross motor skills—and a daily aide. I was taken aback. Why would he need all these supports? Then the words that came out of the speech language pathologist's mouth stopped me dead in my tracks. We were told that JSS was functioning at the level of a one-and-a-half-year-old. He needed ongoing and intensive intervention. We were told that he may have autism and that a multidisciplinary team would be able to help us. In addition, we were told that we would also benefit from seeing a developmental pediatrician at the Child Development Centre at the Alberta Children's Hospital.

Time stood still. I was in shock. I thought to myself, "How can this be? He said 'hi' when we asked him to, and I had been working so hard with him at home. Why? Why my child? Why us? This can't be happening. I will help him, and he won't have autism."

At the time, I was completely unaware that this was the beginning of a journey that would change my life forever . . . for the better.

CHAPTER 5
The Journey Begins

Uncertainty

"Uncertainty filled my life,
I had no words to say;
The pressure of being a Mother
Overpowered me every day.

How would I overcome this challenge?
What would a new day bring?

I needed the strength to go on,
Not live in stress and fear;
Circumstances were so unfair,
For my child who I held so dear."

Mandeep K. Atwal
November 3, 2021

I ARRIVED AT HOME THAT DAY WITHOUT ANY MEMORY OF how I actually drove home. I was so engrossed with the words I had heard. I was numb—I was in a state of shock. I looked through the brochures that the speech therapist had given to us. They were all brochures of organizations that helped children with severe learning needs.

Severe learning needs. These words resonated in my brain, in my mind, and in my soul. My son was considered to have severe learning needs. This wasn't the journey that I had signed up for when I thought about becoming a mother. What had I failed to do as a mother? I had a difficult pregnancy. Had I done something wrong? Did I not feed him the right foods? Did I not stimulate his mind enough?

We didn't know much about autism except for the stereotypes often shown on television and in movies. What would this mean for his life, how would the world treat him, how would we protect him, and what would this mean for our family? These were just a few of the many questions that kept me up at night.

I moved through various stages of anger and sadness, with thoughts like "Why us?" and "Maybe the diagnosis will change" running through my head day and night. I stayed up, night after night, thinking about what the future would hold for us and how I would manage. Every day, I spent hours on the phone with my mom crying and venting. I felt sorry for myself, I felt sorry for JSS, and I resented the situation we found ourselves in. My mom listened to all of my fears and anguish, and she always reassured me that everything would be okay and that there was a reason that God had chosen me for this challenge. She was my rock and my number one cheerleader. I would often tell my mom, after I had vented, that I didn't want her to worry about me. She would respond by saying that my request was impossible for her to fulfill. I still remember her tender, loving voice saying, "Just like you worry about your baby, I worry about my baby." Without her support and encouragement, I know I wouldn't have made it through this time.

I had always been a worrywart, but this truly took my worry to another level. The one good thing was that I wasn't the type of person who would just worry and not take any action to help the situation. I would do both. So as I worried, I also read through all the brochures and tried to find the organization that would best suit our family and best support JSS.

I found an organization called the Cause and Effect Foundation that really spoke to me. They offered individualized programming for children that took place in their natural environments—preschool, home, and the community—in order to help them develop the skills necessary to succeed in each of these environments. I really liked their philosophy of supporting children in their daily environments, thus ensuring natural learning and integration within the community. Under no circumstance was I going to let my son be left behind or not be a part of his school or our community. I spoke with Samir about the Cause and Effect Foundation, and he agreed with me; we were definitely on the same page about which direction we felt was best for JSS.

Samir held in his heart the same passion and fire I had in my soul to help JSS; he was just quieter about it than me. I have always been very sensitive, emotional, and overtly passionate. Although Samir has all these same qualities, he just expresses them in a different way. I was blessed to have Samir to ground me. Within a day, I had called this organization and set up an appointment for two of the directors to come to our home to meet me and JSS.

In June 2009, I met with two of the directors from the Foundation. They also met JSS, and we had a really good conversation. I felt encouraged after speaking with them, and I thought perhaps this was just a temporary condition and that over time, JSS would grow out of it and catch up with his peers. I hoped that maybe he wouldn't have to deal with a diagnosis of autism—and neither would I. After a forty-five-minute meeting with the directors, they indicated that JSS was a good fit for their program and that they would accept him. With the program, an aide under the direction of all of the therapists would come to our home five days a week for three hours. The aide would also accompany JSS to preschool two days a week. A behavioural strategist, a speech language pathologist, an occupational therapist, and a special education teacher would also come to our home on a regular basis to help JSS in all the areas that he needed support.

I was overwhelmed by the thought of having so many people coming in and out of my house. I just wanted a "regular" mom life where I would meet people for playdates and sip coffee as our kids played. I was slowly coming to the realization that my life was taking a very different turn and in no way would my life be "regular" or "typical." As soon as the directors left, I got to work faxing all the relevant documentation to them so we would be ready to start working in September 2009. I immediately called Samir and gave him the good news that our son would be getting the help that he needed and that he would "get better."

JSS's therapy plans were falling into place, and we were establishing our new schedules. Just as I was slowly beginning to reconcile with the fact that I would have to adjust to a very different life than other mothers, I received the devastating news that my mom had been diagnosed with cancer.

My world changed overnight. How could this be happening? I wouldn't survive one day if my mom wasn't here with me. I couldn't even fathom that thought. My mom and I were extremely close; she had me in her early twenties, so we were more like sisters than mother and daughter. And now, hospital visits, chemotherapy, radiation, stem cell transplants, and multiple myeloma became words in my daily vocabulary. Juggling JSS's care and ensuring my mom had what she needed as she struggled with cancer treatments was taking a toll on my soul. My stress and worry levels were through the roof as I dealt with the intensive therapy and interventions that JSS required and the uncertainty of what would happen to my mom. I had already lost touch with the mom friends whom I knew, but now, I was completely isolated. I had no social life or time for myself, as I spent my days taking my mom to the hospital and ensuring that her needs were met, helping members of my extended family, who were also struggling with her diagnosis, and taking care of JSS, who still required a tremendous amount of hands-on care.

I remember coming home from the hospital one day after a three- to four-hour wait for chemotherapy only to listen to JSS cry for an hour and a half. He wasn't used to staying with an extended family member for such a long period of time. Perhaps he was overwhelmed when I came home; maybe his lack of language caused him to react in this way, as he couldn't express how he felt; maybe he was overstimulated; maybe his routine had changed and caused him stress. I didn't understand what was happening. All I knew was that I was completely maxed out, and I didn't know how much more I could take. I was entirely unaware that the next three years were going to be some of the most difficult years of my life, ones I wouldn't wish upon anyone.

The summer of 2009 was manageable with respect to scheduling, as JSS had not started his therapies yet; however, once September hit, I felt like I was on a spinning top. I had people in and out of my house every day for JSS's therapies. JSS had also started preschool, and this was a huge transition for him, as he had to learn how to engage in socially appropriate behaviours, feed himself a snack and deal with the textures of foods on his own, and self-regulate in an overstimulating preschool environment. Without any language, it was going to be extremely difficult for him not to get frustrated and lash out. No one truly understood his wants and needs like me and Samir did.

The food issue really concerned me, as I fed JSS every meal and he had to have his food cut into bite-size pieces so he wouldn't choke. He actually refused to bite into food, like a piece of toast, and he hated the sensation of any food on his fingers and would immediately wipe his fingers if any food got on his hands. We had never gone out anywhere without his food packed with us. How I envied those parents who would buy French fries and just hand them to their kids as they splattered ketchup on them and stuffed them in their mouths. JSS had to work ten times harder just to eat, play, and socialize.

Unlike a regular preschool experience, almost every activity and inter-action was dictated by an Individualized Program Plan, or IPP, which documented JSS's progress at school, at home, and in the community. The IPP was a very important document and necessary to determine the areas that JSS was succeeding in and where he still needed help; however, it com-pletely took away the organic preschool experience for JSS and for me. I wished that I could grab a coffee or even run to the grocery store without worrying about what was happening at preschool, but I was always worried about receiving a phone call that things weren't going well and that it was time to pick him up. I always tried very hard to put aside my worries for a few moments and pray that JSS would meet an IPP goal.

I was so grateful for our aide, Amy, who was a very kind and loving person and had experience with kids who had special needs, specifically autism. At that time, I had still not yet accepted, nor was I ready to accept, that JSS may have autism. I just knew that he needed help to "outgrow" his challenges, and even if someone intimated that he may have autism, I always told myself that my child was different and he did not have and will not have an autism diagnosis. Samir and I weren't against getting the help necessary for JSS, but we weren't even close to accepting that this might be a lifelong condition. I had faith that everything we were doing was going to solve our problems. I continued to think that maybe JSS would outgrow a diagnosis of autism; little did I know that it was me who would grow into it.

I also had faith that my mom was going to be healed. The doctors had told us that they caught the cancer early and that she was eligible for a stem cell transplant, which would take place in November 2009. In preparation for the stem cell transplant, my mom was given a very intense chemotherapy treatment that wiped her immunity clean. As a result, her immune system was very vulnerable, and this meant that she couldn't be around JSS. This broke her heart and mine. They were extremely close, and it was very difficult for JSS to even understand what was happening. All these circumstances weighed heavily on my heart, and I often looked to God and would ask the same questions: "Why? Why me? Why us?"

I spent my days with JSS, his aide, and his therapists, and once Samir was home and could take over, I spent my evenings with my mom. Although I had no time for myself, let alone my marriage, Samir was extremely supportive and never, ever questioned my love for or dedication to my mother. In light of our circumstances, we had to put our relationship on the back burner. However, this didn't cause us to drift apart; in fact, we became closer as we developed a greater mutual respect for each other by witnessing what each of us was prepared to do for the ones we love. Samir's support got me through some very, very tough days.

One cold day in November 2009, as Amy was working with JSS downstairs, I sat in my bedroom trying to get a little rest before I started my next shift reinforcing the new skills that JSS was taught on that day. Generally, I wasn't present for the therapies, as JSS would cry more and break down if he saw me because he was working so hard to acquire the skills that other children developed so naturally. I was his safety net, and although I felt terrible that he was being pushed so hard to learn, I knew that this was the best thing for him. As I was eavesdropping on JSS's therapy that day, I heard Amy repeating words over and over again in an attempt to get JSS to copy her and repeat the words. Over and over, week after week, Amy would try and get JSS to repeat her words. She used many techniques, but still, his vocabulary was very limited. Like all the other days, when I listened in on what was happening, I waited, and I prayed. Please, JSS, just say the words. Please.

All of a sudden, I heard JSS repeat the word that Amy said. I heard sheer excitement in Amy's voice as she started to say more words: "Book, shelf, counter, cabinet, milk, juice, picture!" And then, JSS was repeating all these words—it was happening! I listened with a huge smile on my face, love in my heart, and tears streaming down my face. JSS also caught Amy's excitement, and he began repeating all the words with the same enthusiasm. My boy, who some thought might never speak, was repeating every word he was hearing. It was through our hard work and the grace of God that this day had finally come. I could barely contain my excitement as I called Samir at work and told him the good news.

I gave JSS the biggest hug and kiss that day. I was so proud of him for working so hard. I continued with the repetition of words for the rest of the day, and the next, and the next. Once again, on that day, I felt my fatigue and weakness turn into strength. Our determination was paying off, and I felt like we had put another drop of strength in our bucket. Actually, on that day, our bucket felt completely full of strength.

As we forged ahead with this newfound strength, I became more aware of the inequities that existed in the world for a child living with special needs or autism. I was told by the preschool that if Amy was sick or unable to attend preschool with JSS, he couldn't attend unless I accompanied him. JSS had a lot of energy and was very inquisitive, but in no way did he demonstrate aggressive or violent behaviour. I questioned this decision and even suggested that I could pick him up if they weren't able to support him; however, I was told there was no choice, and either I attended with him or we would have to wait until Amy was back. There was an assumption that he couldn't manage without his aide, even though children with autism often thrived in routine-driven environments.

This was my first real exposure to JSS being denied an opportunity to attend school due to his unique learning needs, and this made me angry. In my mind, I questioned why more preschools didn't receive training in how to teach children with autism. We had sent JSS to this preschool so he could be integrated in a "typical" learning environment, learn from his peers, and develop the skills and social habits that other people modelled in front of him. We were told many times that exposure to daily learning environments and other children was the key in helping a child with autism, especially at a young age. We weren't going to let JSS miss even one day of learning and potential growth, so I gave up my only break in the week from therapies and training and attended preschool with JSS on the days Amy couldn't.

Although Samir and I were still not prepared to accept the fact that JSS might have a diagnosis of autism, there was no way we were going to deny him the therapies and interventions that he needed in case we were wrong. In 2009, the autism spectrum wasn't very broad, and a child had to fit into certain categories in order to receive a diagnosis of autism. Even though JSS exhibited a language delay and typical sensory regulation behaviours of those with autism, he didn't exhibit the expected lack of interest in social interactions. He was extremely social and loved meeting people and playing with children. His behaviour wasn't always socially appropriate, though, as he often hugged and squeezed children out of sheer excitement whether they liked it or not; however, he didn't feel uncomfortable in social situations and interactions or avoid them in the least.

The reason for our hesitancy in accepting a diagnosis of autism for JSS wasn't due to how it might make us feel or what our family and friends might think—it was more of a deep-rooted fear of how the world would view and treat our son. The thought that he would be denied opportunities and be ostracized due to his diagnosis was a thought we weren't able to bear. Therefore, we continued receiving all the help that we could for him while holding off on pursuing any sort of formal diagnosis.

The first year of JSS's preschool and therapies was a frenzy of activity. Every day, JSS would be busy working hard and learning new skills. I continued to meet with therapists and implement the techniques and strategies they told me would best suit JSS and his development. With my legal training, it was natural for me to research everything about autism. After I would finish my research about autism and reflect upon how it could possibly affect JSS and our family, I would cry and then I would pray. "Please, God," I would say, "not us." Thinking of JSS struggling in his life kept me up at night. I thought about how difficult life would be for him if he received a diagnosis of autism.

I also thought about how I had faced racism growing up and how I was able to overcome many of the cruel comments and behaviour I had to endure because of my understanding of the language and my ability to advocate for myself and fight back. My willpower and tenacity helped me deal with some very heartbreaking situations. With expressive and receptive language delays being JSS's main challenges, if he found himself being challenged or bullied, how would he stand up for himself in life? Autism would add another layer of hardship to these types of challenges.

Almost every night, when JSS would finally fall asleep, I would sneak into his room and sit on the floor by his bed. I would softly touch his face, brush his hair back from his forehead, and hold his hand. I would look at him sleeping and think about how peaceful and normal everything seemed. I would whisper to him how much I loved him and how I wanted to take away any pain or hardship in his life and make it my burden, not his. My heart absolutely ached for him, and I questioned why he had to go through all this. This wasn't the journey we expected to take when we thought about our family and our kids. I cried so much I thought I had no more tears to cry, but every night, as I sat by his bed, my soul would find more tears, and they would well up and roll down my cheeks like a fountain full of love and pain.

The year 2010 allowed me to focus a little more on JSS, as my mom's stem cell transplant in November 2009 was a success. Aside from a few appointments here and there, the gruelling physical and mental pain of my mom's chemotherapy treatments and hospital visits were beginning to subside. I was extremely relieved and thankful to God for healing my mom. The thought of going through my struggles with JSS without her support was unimaginable for me. In June 2010, we moved into a new home. This was only possible as my mom's follow-up appointments were decreasing, and I had a couple of hours, two times a week, to pack and move things into our new home while JSS was in preschool with Amy.

In August 2010, we were able to book an appointment with a developmental pediatrician at the Alberta Children's Hospital whom JSS's pediatrician referred to us. We were looking forward to this appointment, as it would give us some concrete answers with respect to how JSS was progressing and whether we were doing enough to help him. During our journey, we were blessed to have amazing doctors helping JSS. JSS's pediatrician was a godsend, and she always gave us the support and resources we needed and listened to our concerns with great patience, genuine concern, and compassion. She knew we were both lawyers and therefore inherently very thorough researchers, so we would always come in with a million questions and a ton of research in hand. JSS's pediatrician was never, ever dismissive; she always validated our concerns and feelings, and she never pushed us to just accept a diagnosis of autism. The way she treated JSS showed us that she loved her job and the children under her medical care. It's not easy to find doctors with these qualities, and we will never forget how she supported and encouraged us, and how she continues to do so to this day. We were happy to meet the developmental pediatrician because we quickly recognized that he had the same passion for his job and respect for our views as JSS's pediatrician.

As I mentioned earlier, at the time of our meeting with the developmental pediatrician, the autism spectrum wasn't as broad as it is today, and people with autism were expected to exhibit certain characteristics, some of which included a speech language delay, a lack of interest in socializing, sensory regulation difficulties, stimming (repetitive movements or noises), repetitive speech patterns, and hyperfocusing on preferred areas of interest. After meeting with the developmental pediatrician and providing him with all the relevant information, including the many forms we had completed, we were told that although JSS exhibited many of the typical traits associated with autism, the fact that he was so extremely social made it difficult for JSS to receive an official diagnosis.

In all honesty, I was relieved, as I felt that I still had the chance to help JSS so he could live and function as a "typically developing" child and adult. I wasn't at a point of acceptance where I could stand on the mountaintop and yell, "My son has autism, and I'm ready to face the world!" In fact, the thought of an autism diagnosis made me want to crawl into my bed and cry in my mother's arms. However, regardless of a diagnosis, we were trying to be very objective and logical, and we knew JSS still needed a lot of support. We asked the developmental pediatrician, "If we assume that JSS does have autism, what supports would he continue to benefit from?" We never, ever wanted to look back with regret and feel that we didn't help our son in the best way possible. Our fear had always been the stigma that a diagnosis of autism would carry as JSS navigated the school system and the world. Autism or not, he was our precious child, and we were prepared to go to the ends of the earth to help him.

After receiving the information on all the support he would still require, we knew we had a long road ahead. Amid my anguish and thoughts about the long journey ahead of us, I considered it a blessing and a huge asset that Samir and I were lawyers. This definitely helped us navigate the many hoops we had to jump through to ensure that JSS received the support he needed and deserved. Effectively communicating with many agencies and medical professionals, understanding contracts, becoming familiar with administrative processes and appeals, and having thorough research skills were all vital in successfully advocating for our son. I thought about the people who were new immigrants to this country and how complex and confusing the system must be for them. I wished I could help each and every one of them so their children could also get the support that they required and deserved. We felt so overwhelmed trying to get JSS the supports that he needed, and we were born, raised, and educated in Canada. I couldn't even imagine how people in more challenging circumstances felt.

Right then, there was a very small shift in me. Not one that would be noticeable to anyone, but for the first time, I was thankful for something in this taxing, overwhelming journey—our ability to advocate for JSS.

CHAPTER 6

Light at the End of the Tunnel

———

Prayer for My Mother

*"I have to confess; over the past nine years, I have
wandered this earth looking for you,*

*Hoping that if I turn a certain corner, you will
be there smiling at me,
Ready to hug me and tell me that everything
is going to be okay.*

*I have to confess; I have played that day
over in my head a million times,
Wondering if I could have done something to stop time
to keep you with me a little longer.*

*I have to confess; there is an emptiness in
my heart that will always be there.
My soul longs to see you, to hear your voice,
For us to be together again.*

*I will wait for that day, but until then,
I will make you proud and do the best I can for my family,
Just like you did for me.*

*Love you from the depths of my soul, Mama.
Miss you in my life.*

Love, your daughter,
Mandy"

Mandeep K. Atwal
January 17, 2021

IN THE FALL OF 2010, I HAD BEGUN TO SEE A SMALL LIGHT AT the end of the tunnel—a renewed sense of hope. JSS had not been diagnosed with autism, and my mom was in remission.

This light was quickly extinguished when we received the news that my mom's cancer had returned after only approximately three months in remission. I was once more immersed in a whirlwind of confusion and stress. Chemotherapy, radiation, hospital visits, and the stress of seeing my best friend in pain again overpowered my life. At that time, I still truly believed that this was all temporary and that Mom would be in remission again very soon. My soul couldn't bear thinking any other way. I had to live in faith, not fear.

Therapy sessions for JSS continued in my home, and every day I pushed him to continue to learn and do a little more than he did the day before. We added physiotherapy to his regime, which took place once a week or so in a gym outside of the home. We undertook physiotherapy for JSS in order to help him with his motor planning and to decrease the rigidity of some of his movements. We also worked on daily living skills such as independently dressing and eating. All of these challenges were exacerbated by the fact that JSS's language was limited and he couldn't explain how he felt or what he needed.

JSS had never been a great sleeper, but he was sleeping better throughout the night as we started giving him melatonin after our visit with the developmental pediatrician. With a good night's sleep, it seemed as though JSS's language was getting a little better, as he was able to focus more during the day. Prior to giving him melatonin, JSS would wake up in the middle of night and talk to himself for two or three hours, often in words and sentences that didn't make sense to me—it sounded like gibberish. Obviously, this was very worrisome to Samir and me, and we were relieved when this decreased and we were all able to sleep a little better at night. These few adjustments made a big difference in our lives and allowed me to be there for my mom when she needed me.

I often thought about having another baby. I knew that JSS was lonely and that he would love to have a sibling. He spent most of his time with adults—either his parents or his therapists who would be teaching him new skills. I knew that having the chance to interact with another child in our home and developing a new relationship with a sibling would make him very happy. However, I knew this wasn't the right time because of my current responsibilities, the very real possibility of getting as sick as I did with my first pregnancy, and possibly facing major complications again during my delivery.

The real focus of this year had been preparation for the fall of 2011, when JSS would begin kindergarten. We had some big decisions to make. Questions filled our minds and our daily discussions. Would we send him to a special education school? Would we have to share all of the details of his challenges with a "regular" school and risk the stigma that others may attach to these challenges, or would he improve so much by the time kindergarten started that this would be unnecessary? Were we moving further away from a diagnosis of autism with all the help he was getting? Although JSS was repeating many words now, he still had tremendous difficulty constructing a lot of sentences. He still flapped his arms in excitement and would often engage in repetitive movements as a way to express how he felt, whether it be excitement, anxiety, or frustration.

Little things to which other children may not have given a second thought would often entertain JSS. He loved to watch those flexible metal doorstoppers vibrate after he would hit them; if he saw a vacuum anywhere, he would just have to play with it; and he could watch the garage door open and close for an hour. This definitely made coming into the house a challenge, as we had to set a limit on the number of times we could open and close the garage door. I had to put up a printed "social story" on the wall in our mudroom with a sequence of events explaining to JSS how many times the door could be opened and closed. We had actually been using social stories for the last two years to explain many different aspects of life to JSS, such as the steps necessary in brushing your teeth, getting ready in the morning for school, making friends, identifying emotions, waiting patiently, expressing your needs—the list was endless. As one may expect, these booklets were all over my house, and they would help JSS create and learn to live with routines and structure, which caused him less stress and anxiety. Although we tried to stick to our social stories and routines the best that we could, everything didn't always go so smoothly, and daily meltdowns were a part of life.

I continued to test JSS to see where he was developmentally. These weren't formal tests found in child development books; these were a concerned mother's tests. I always wanted to find success in JSS and then be able to prove everyone wrong. I would sit down with JSS and encourage him to ask me to play. This would help him develop his language skills and his social interaction skills. I remember sitting down on the floor with JSS one day and just waiting for him to ask me to play. He picked up a car and handed it to me and said, "Mama feed." I was stunned. I knew what he meant, but why was he saying "Mama feed" and not "Mama play"?

I wanted to break down. Was I getting anywhere? What was happening? Was I expecting too much? A million thoughts raced through my head as I looked at my son waiting to play with me. Anxiety, fear, and stress filled my body and mind. I knew that in this situation, using words alone wasn't going to help him. I needed to demonstrate to him what he was saying; he was a visual learner. So I took the car from him and pretended to feed it to him. He started laughing and was amused and shocked by what I was doing. I said, "Okay, Mama feed." He was perplexed and he said, "No." I then said to him, "Mama play?" He kept laughing and repeated, "Mama play." JSS thought I was just joking around, and he was smiling and laughing—so happy, so innocent and so perfect.

I was scared—scared of how cruel the world could be to such an innocent soul. Thinking about this injustice fired up my spirit. I wanted my son to be able to take care of himself and fight for himself. To advocate for his rights and be treated with respect and kindness. I feared his innocence would be his greatest detriment. I kept these fears and worries deep in my heart, and I continued to make inroads. I would never give up, and I knew, just like a mama bear, I was ready to attack anyone who would even dream of hurting him.

The days turned to weeks, the weeks turned to months, and in what seemed to be a blink of an eye, we were wrapping up JSS's second year of therapy. On the other hand, my mom had been in and out of the hospital since September 2010, and she still wasn't feeling well. We couldn't understand why, after all of her treatments, things weren't getting better. The situation went from bad to worse in May 2011. My mom was very dizzy, nauseated, and suffering from severe headaches. We were at a loss as to what was happening. She lived in a city three hours away from us, and all her chemotherapy and radiation treatments had occurred in Calgary. At the end of May 2011, my mom came to Calgary in preparation for an appointment that she had at the Tom Baker Cancer Centre to try and figure out what was happening.

June 3, 2011 was by far the worst day of my life. We received the news that the cancer had spread to my mom's brain. She only had six weeks left to live. I felt like someone had taken a gun and shot me in the heart. I couldn't breathe. I couldn't think. I was thankful that JSS was in preschool when I received the news; I was at home alone. I collapsed to the ground and completely broke down. I was crying, screaming, and yelling at God, "Why my mom? Why?!" Out of nowhere, the sky filled with clouds, and there was a tremendous boom of thunder louder than I had ever heard before in my life. It was as if the sky was screaming and crying with me.

After I pulled myself together, my faith took over. I knew that God would hear my prayers and that my mom would see a miracle. There was no way I was going to accept defeat. That was just not my nature. If someone told me I couldn't do something, it would push me even harder to prove them wrong. My mom was also a very strong and positive person, and she never gave up. During the summer of 2011, I spent as much time as I could with my mom, bringing JSS with me whenever possible. The doctors didn't have much hope, but I just knew that my mom would be healed. She would be cured. She would be the miracle story that everyone would talk about. The doctors had only given her six weeks to live in June; however, she had defied the odds and was still with us in September 2011.

JSS's therapies ended in June 2011 for the summer, and we prepared for kindergarten. We had to make some tough decisions. JSS was still facing many challenges, and it was evident we would have to share all his challenges with the school in order for him to receive the support he needed. We decided to send JSS into the "regular stream" for schooling, as he had done so well in preschool learning and observing children who were engaging in "typical" social interactions. We felt this environment best suited JSS, as it pushed him to improve and further develop his skills.

Our time with the Cause and Effect Foundation had come to an end, but we were able to access the services of another organization with a multidisciplinary team. The Ability Society of Alberta would support JSS every day after school, and the structure was very similar to the Cause and Effect Foundation. Even though I still felt a little demoralized that I wasn't able to help JSS "catch up" before kindergarten, I recognized that we were blessed to be receiving this help. I kept on pushing forward and thinking about all the gains he would make in this next year and how he would be right on track by grade 1.

Unfortunately, my mom's health took a turn for the worse in November 2011, and she ended up back in the hospital. The woman who once was so full of life and energy was lying in a hospital bed, unable to move. This completely crushed me, and I felt like I didn't have any direction; there was nowhere I could turn and nothing I could do. I was completely helpless. This was an unbearable time. I would spend as much time at the hospital as I could, talking to doctors and ensuring that Mom received the best care possible, while at the same time trying to balance my responsibilities as a mother and a wife. Many times, I would spend the night at the hospital and then come home in the morning just in time for Samir to go work and for the therapists and aide to come and help JSS. I was completely exhausted—emotionally and physically. I wasn't sleeping at all, and the mental stress of watching my mom suffer was killing my soul. I was dragging myself through life and being kicked as I tried to crawl forward through some very dark days. I wasn't myself at all. Everything in my life that wasn't my mom or JSS was on the back burner. If it wasn't for Samir's support, I wouldn't have survived during this time.

One day in December 2011, when I was picking up JSS from school, his kindergarten teacher came out and congratulated me on being pregnant. I was shocked and told her I wasn't expecting. She said, "Oh, JSS said that he was going to have a baby sister." I laughed and thought about what a great story JSS told his teacher, and I didn't really think about it again. But it reminded me of one day in July 2011 when I was praying, and a beautiful baby girl's name came to me. I had shared this name with my mom and told her that if I ever have a girl, I would give her this name. My mom loved the name. One December evening at the hospital in 2011, my mom told me that she wanted me to have another baby. I told her I wanted her to get better first. She said, "No, don't wait."

On January 21, 2012, I said goodbye to my best friend and number one supporter—my mother. I always thought that if I lost my mom, I wouldn't be able to go on for even one day. I confided in her about everything, and we had a very special and close mother-daughter relationship. As I held my mom's hand for the last time and kissed her cheek, I told her how much I loved her, how much I would miss her, and how I would do everything to support my children just as she had done for me. I said goodbye to that part of my childhood that only a parent can remind you of, to that place where you can always come to feel safe and free. I thought to myself that if I could become even half of the woman that she was, I would consider myself a successful human being. The only thing that gave me solace in this time of complete devastation was my knowledge that she was no longer suffering or in pain.

Four days after my mom passed away, I found out I was expecting my second child. As I delivered my mom's eulogy, I could feel her standing right next to me, supporting me, comforting me, and telling me that a very special gift from God would be blessing my life. An angel would be sent to help me heal and go on.

My second child was born nine months later, and JSS was right—he was going to have a baby sister. He had this knowledge months before any of us did.

"Mom, my heart still aches for you,
But my soul knows you are still with me."

CHAPTER 7
"Shakti," *Divine Power*

Prayer for My Children on the First Day of School

"A new year has begun, and I wave and watch you go;
Only my heart knows my worry, as I walk away so slow.

It seems like only yesterday you were babies in my arms,
And now I have to worry about all the worldly harms.

I pray with all my heart that you are happy and content,
And if you need some help or love, that God's angels will be sent.

You are my precious children—I can't always be around,
But remember, if you ever need me, in your heart I'm
always found.

Love, Mom xoxo"

Mandeep K. Atwal
September 2, 2019

I WAS DEALING WITH A TREMENDOUS AMOUNT OF GRIEF
after losing my mom, but I was also so severely sick during my pregnancy
that I spent almost all of my time in bed. I only got the strength to get out
of bed when I had to speak to JSS's therapists, who were still coming to help
JSS in our home, and when I had to get up to make JSS his meals. Other
than that, I had a hard time even making it down the stairs. Naturally, with

no help and a child with special needs, it was one of the most difficult times of my life. I would sit and think, "Are things ever going to get better?" I was facing one obstacle after another with no reprieve. Alongside the stress of raising a child with special needs and managing a pregnancy where I could barely get out of bed, I also worried about possible complications during the delivery. I had a real fear of dying due to what happened during my first delivery. The stakes were much higher now, as I knew that JSS needed me, and I thought, "If something happened to me, what would happen to him?" I tried to think positively, but I was scared. I knew that anything was possible after I saw what happened to me when I was giving birth to JSS.

In addition to these worries, I also often bore criticism from some family members that I was wasting my legal education by deciding to stay at home with my kids and not going back to work. This was very hard to hear, especially since I already asked myself this question many times. I would look up to God and ask him why I had spent so many years in university training to be a lawyer only to be in this situation. I still didn't truly appreciate how my legal education had played, and was going to play, a vital role in how I cared for and advocated for my son. At this point in my life, I didn't trust my soul journey and my soul lessons in the manner I should have, but over time, with experience, I would gain this trust in myself and my journey.

Life went on. The challenges we faced piled up like weights upon our souls. JSS was never able to use toothpaste with fluoride, as he didn't understand that he couldn't swallow it and had to spit it out. Therefore, we always brushed his teeth with toothpaste that didn't contain fluoride, and we were very diligent in taking him to the dentist regularly. However, this lack of fluoride in his toothpaste caught up with us, and in May 2012, JSS had to have dental surgery. He was put under anaesthesia for the surgery, and needless to say, this was an extremely stressful event for all of us. I still don't know how I sat in the surgery unit for eight hours, pregnant and extremely sick, waiting for JSS to have his surgery. It was overwhelmingly stressful knowing that JSS didn't truly understand what was going on, and I would have to watch him being put under while he was screaming and reaching out for me. I was a mess. I didn't know how much more I could take.

Amid all of this anguish and stress, a part of me was always mindful of the fact that God and my mom were sending me angels as a way to lift me up during these very trying times. JSS's aide at school, Margie, was truly a godsend. JSS really connected with her, and she was very empathetic to my struggles of being so sick and having just lost my mom. Without Margie's support, life would have been extremely difficult. I couldn't always be there for JSS the way I wanted to, and I was very grateful for the love and support Margie gave my son at school.

Equally, our aide through the at-home support program, Jessica, was a blessing. She helped JSS understand why I was so sick and helped him cope with his confusion. She was extremely empathetic to our situation, and she did everything she could to make our journey a little easier. JSS was only five years old, and with an expressive and receptive language delay, one can only imagine how extremely difficult it was for him to process what had happened to his grandmother and what was happening to his mom. JSS would say to me, "What's wrong, Mama?" and "Get up!" When I told him there was a baby in my tummy and I was very sick, he asked me if I was going to die like Grandma. As I looked at my little boy, I felt so sad that he had these feelings in his heart. I know it must have taken a lot for him to express this thought, as he hadn't truly understood where his grandma had gone and when she would be back. I remember him looking for her under the covers of her bed after she had passed away. His innocence was a stark reminder to me of how vulnerable he might be in our world.

On September 16, 2012, my baby girl, AKS, was born, and I gave her the name that I shared with my mom months before I was even expecting her. "Noble woman" is the meaning of her name, and that is exactly who she is. AKS came to me as my *Shakti*, a word which means divine power in Sanskrit and represents the dynamic forces that move through the entire universe.[2] She would prove this over and over again in the years that followed by supporting us and becoming an advocate for those with special needs. She was a gift from God and my mom's message to me that love truly transcends the physical plane. AKS brought a piece of heaven, and a piece of my mom, to earth for me during a very difficult and desperate

---

2   "Shakti," Wikiquote, last modified May 6, 2022, https://en.wikiquote.org/wiki/Shakti.

time. For one moment in time, all the physical and emotional hardships I faced during the nine months before AKS was born were worth it.

As JSS transitioned into grade 1, we continued to do everything we could to help him advance and succeed. We continued with aide support and speech therapy at school. At home, we had a behavioural strategist, an occupational therapist, and a speech language pathologist continue to support JSS, along with our amazing new aide, Stephanie, who would come every day after school to help us implement the strategies that were recommended. We were blessed to have another loving and compassionate aide like Stephanie come into our home. It didn't take long for both JSS and AKS to become extremely attached to Stephanie, and just like our previous aide, Jessica, she became a member of our family.

Doctors' visits for both children became a regular part of life. Terms like weighted vests, ABA therapy, speech delay, ADHD, government funding, disability, special needs, fine motor skills, gross motor skills, stimming, echolalia, etc., would swirl around in my head constantly and became a part of our daily vocabulary. Still, I wasn't entirely ready to hear and accept the word autism. Everything that we could do, we did—all while raising a newborn and grieving the loss of my mom.

I spent my days worrying about things that perhaps didn't cross the minds of many others. JSS had a hard time understanding when it was hot and cold outside and how many layers of clothing he would need. He needed someone to tell him what he needed to wear when he went outside. I would be sitting at home feeding AKS and thinking, "Was someone helping him and protecting him at school?" Even things like understanding when he was hungry didn't come easily for JSS. I always made sure he was fed on time, had a routine, and actually ate his meals. I had to keep track of all this because it was like he didn't understand the cues and signals his body was giving him.

I later learned that this was exactly what was happening. I learned that we have eight senses, not five. One of these additional senses is called interoception, which is the "sense that allows us to feel sensations from inside of our bodies."[3] It's a "connection between the mind and the body."[4] Interoception is the ability, or lack thereof, to understand the physical cues that your body gives you about how you're feeling.[5] Typically, children with autism have a hard time understanding these signals.

Although I appreciated this newfound knowledge on interoception, it still did not ease my worries. JSS was in school full-time and away from me all day long. It continued to be a very trying time. I found joy in the little moments, like when JSS would rush to me after school to see his little sister and give her a kiss. He adored her, and even though she was just a little baby, I could see the twinkle in her eyes when she saw her big brother. It was like they just understood each other and loved each other. I never wanted their bond to be broken, and I wanted AKS to be his number one advocate in life. Time would show me that she exceeded this hope in every respect.

School pickup times were difficult for me and had been difficult ever since preschool. Many of the moms became friends over the years and spent time catching up before the dismissal bell. My life was different. JSS was different. I had spent the last three years trying to keep up with JSS after school as he ran around or was upset at the end of the day from too much sensory stimulation or overload. Often, his aide at school, Margie, would come out to let me know how the day went, and the looks from some of the other moms had judgment written all over it. Looking away from my child, even for a second, wasn't an option. He didn't understand danger or appropriate socialization in the same way as other children. I was always worried about him saying or doing the wrong thing and about others negatively judging him. The thought of anyone looking down on my child or considering him less in any way was unbearable to me. Some of the stares I received clearly told me what some of the parents thought of JSS and me.

3   Kelly Mahler, "What exactly is Interoception?" Kelly Mahler, May 10, 2022, https://www.kelly-mahler.com/resources/blog/what-exactly-is-interoception.
4   Mahler, "What exactly is Interoception?"
5   Kelly Mahler and Bud Craig, *Interoception: The Eighth Sensory System* (Lenexa: AAPC Publishing, 2015).

Therefore, I didn't have a lot of friends at school, but we held our own. I wanted my children to see that being different was okay, and that this should be a source of pride and confidence, although I did go home and sometimes wish that more people at school understood what I was going through and maybe even offered me a helping hand. I felt sad some days and angry on others. There were a few moms who were always nice to me, and I appreciated their care and consideration. Looking back now, I realize that although some looks we got from parents were clearly judgmental, others may have been looking at us trying to understand JSS's behaviour or wondering why he was doing the things that he was, or perhaps they didn't know how to help when we were having a rough day. All I know is that I promised myself I would never let JSS be treated poorly, and I would always make sure that any mom or child that I met would be included, receive confidence, and gain strength from me.

These experiences helped me teach my children that it's better to be alone and have your dignity than to be around people who don't respect you. It also helped me teach them that for every judgmental person you meet, there will be another person around the corner who is not judgmental and is, in fact, supportive. I reinforced to my children the importance of not letting the negative people or bullies get you down. They aren't the ones you learn from and definitely not the ones you model. You have to have faith in who you are and be true to yourself. You have your own unique power and strength. By believing in yourself, you are showing the world your belief in its goodness. It becomes a vibration with an extremely far-reaching impact.

JSS had a hard time sitting in class, and we often received calls from the school about the disruption he had caused. I was so thankful for Margie, who was like an angel sent from my mom to not only support JSS, but to encourage me and reassure me that everything was going to be okay. She focused on the positive, and this really helped me regroup and stay on track. I was so exhausted all the time, as AKS didn't sleep at all, and it took all my energy to focus on and understand what the school was saying to me and to keep up with the strategies of the aide and therapists that were still coming to our home to help JSS. I remember days where I would be up with AKS all night and not sleep a wink, send JSS to school, and then, in the same clothes I slept in, sit down for a meeting at our home with four or five therapists to discuss the progress JSS was making and what he required to continue succeeding.

Please don't misunderstand me—I was thankful for all the help we were receiving, but I was totally depleted. At times, I felt completely alone, as we didn't have any friends who also had a child with special needs with whom we could share our joys and pains, and without my mom's support and physical help, there were many days I felt utterly helpless. I had no time for myself. That successful, well-dressed lawyer I saw in my dreams as a child and my previous life in Toronto as a criminal and immigration lawyer seemed like distant memories. I wondered when my life would change for the better, if ever.

As other kids in the neighbourhood would play outside after supper, I watched as my six-year-old son sat at a table with his dad learning, repeating, and writing words. Samir is an amazing father, and I am so thankful for his presence in our lives. He would work long days as a lawyer and then come home to support our family in any way he could. I know he felt the same stress that I did about JSS's future, but he carried it in a very graceful way. As I watched them work, I would think to myself, "I have never seen a little boy work so hard." JSS was and still is resilient. After a full day of school, and then two hours of work at home with Stephanie, our little boy would continue to persevere. I ached for him. I ached for me. I ached for our family. However, over time, I realized that by watching him struggle and work ten times harder than a "typically" developing child, I wasn't helping him navigate his spiritual journey; rather, he was helping me. He was changing me. He was changing our family.

CHAPTER 8

Power and Strength in Acceptance

"Rise up and Raise Up."

Mandeep K. Atwal
October 2021

OUR DAYS WERE VERY LONG, BUT THE YEARS FLEW BY. BEFORE we knew it, JSS was almost done grade 1, and AKS was almost a year old. AKS had become accustomed to the aides and therapists coming in and out of our house. She was actually very excited whenever they came because she thought we had "playdates" and "friends" coming over every day. It was the most exciting part of the day for her. Her sweet and innocent soul didn't understand the hard work that JSS was engaging in every day to try and learn the skills that other children learned so naturally.

Samir and I worried about AKS. Would she also have to face the developmental challenges that JSS was facing? How could I possibly handle two children with learning challenges? How would I manage without my mom? We were offered the option of undertaking genetic testing before AKS was even conceived to determine the likelihood of any of our future children having autism, but we declined. I had faith that the journey that God had chosen for me was one that I could handle and one that I was meant to pursue.

My thinking has changed a little now; rather than "accepting" my journey, I believe my soul chose my journey even before I was born. It wasn't God's decision; it was mine. I chose to learn valuable lessons in this life in order for my soul to grow. The first lesson was unconditional love. There wasn't anything in this world Samir and I wouldn't do for JSS. I was prepared to give up every one of my needs to ensure he had everything he needed. He was my son, and I was his mother. I took great pride and honour in having this responsibility. I brought him into this world, and I would make sure that this world treated him fairly and that he would have every tool necessary in order to succeed. Giving up and failure were never options.

We rejoiced in the small victories, like JSS learning to tie his shoelaces and zipping up his coat. Although the motor skills necessary to engage in activities like riding a bike were very difficult for JSS, we were more focused on, and amazed by, his special abilities. On one occasion, his aide asked me to come into our playroom/teaching room, and she pointed to our chalk board where JSS had written, completely independently, numbers going up by fours well into the thousands range. I was shocked, as in school, they had only learned to count to twenty or so. He also started building complex Lego on his own and taking apart clocks and watches and putting everything back together again.

He also had this unique and amazing ability to predict whether someone was having a baby boy or a baby girl. To this day, he has never had an incorrect prediction. Many of my friends have loved receiving this secret information from JSS, much as I did when he predicted the birth of his baby sister months before I was even expecting. I recall asking him when he was young how he knew the gender of the baby when the baby was still in the mother's tummy. He very nonchalantly told me, "I can see the baby." I just left it at that. It seemed like the world was always focusing on his "deficiencies," but I saw his strengths. His brain worked uniquely, and this wasn't bad or worse—it was just different. He learned in a different way and saw the world in a different way. Why is the "neurotypical" way the "only" way? It isn't. Not for us. So we continued helping JSS learn the skills he needed to progress in this world, but we also began to appreciate the differences that made him powerful and unique.

Regular visits to his doctors and filling out numerous forms and questionnaires about his successes and his challenges became a part of our daily life. In April 2013, JSS's pediatrician and developmental pediatrician observed him in his grade 1 classroom in order to see how he engaged in everyday school-related tasks. Socialization skills, academic comprehension, self-regulation, overall behaviour, and his ability to focus in class were all key components of the observation. We felt it was very important that this observation take place, as it gave the doctors the opportunity to observe JSS in a natural setting and not just in the context of a medical appointment. We knew that the main reason for the observation was to determine whether a diagnosis of autism should or could be made at this time. For many years, JSS had been receiving all the support and intervention that would have been necessary for a child who had a diagnosis of autism. As time went on and we moved away from looking at JSS through the subjective eyes of loving and protective parents, we began to see what was there. We were still loving and protective parents, but our lens shifted to one that was more objective.

After the observation, we all had a meeting in the front office of the school. Samir, seven-month-old AKS in her stroller and cookie in hand, and I were ready to hear what the doctors had to say. The doctors told us all about their observations and the manner in which JSS was communicating, interacting, and learning within the school environment. Close to the end of the session, one of the doctors looked at us and told us in a very supportive manner that after the observation that day, the consensus was that JSS had autism spectrum disorder and attention deficit hyperactivity disorder (ADHD).

When I heard those words, I wasn't broken, shocked, or hurt—for the first time, I was at peace. We had been working to help JSS for the last five years on the assumption that he had autism so as not to deprive him of any therapy, opportunity, or help that he may need in the early years. Now, I was at a point of acceptance. I didn't realize that with this acceptance came a tremendous amount of power and strength; in fact, I was about to find out how powerful we would become. Feeling empowered after hearing those words wasn't the reaction I was expecting. This was my journey, and I was ready to embrace it with strength, self-confidence, and pride. I thought about my son and what a wonderful person he was, how proud I was to be his mom, and how I would do everything in my power to support him throughout his life. I could feel my son's heart, and I felt completely in tune with him. Now my passion wasn't just to help him, but also to help others learn about him and appreciate his strengths and abilities. Samir and I were both on the same page, and we walked out of that meeting with a strength that radiated from our souls.

In June 2013, the official diagnosis letter came in the mail, along with a stack of material on how to access supports for those living with autism. My complete acceptance and strength came at the perfect time because as JSS was getting older, so were the kids at school, and they began to really see that he was different. JSS needed me to be strong and supportive now more than ever. With the realization that JSS was different, a few kids were ready to help, but as we expected, some saw him as weak and naïve, and the bullying began.

Other factors exacerbated the situation. JSS had always had a difficult time sitting still in class and focusing on his schoolwork. With his autism diagnosis came a diagnosis of ADHD, and we began to understand why he had such a hard time focusing. Samir and I discussed giving him prescription medication for the ADHD on multiple occasions, and we were definitely both reluctant. However, after numerous discussions with his doctors, reviewing the feedback from his teachers about how hard it was for him to focus in school, and doing a ton of research, it was with a heavy heart that we started him on a low dose of medication. We tested about four different medications before we decided on one best suited for him. This medication didn't come without its side effects, including difficulty sleeping and a loss of appetite; however, the biggest and most noticeable side effect was the development of tics. It broke our heart to watch JSS with these tics. He was already singled out for being different, and now, we felt that we had added to his challenges. I would sit and think about him and how hard it would be for an eight-year-old child to understand why he was displaying these uncontrollable body and facial movements. I could feel his heart; I could feel his pain.

The lack of invitations to birthday parties and playdates didn't help the situation. This absence of acceptance and understanding hurt my soul, and

I realized I couldn't always protect JSS the way I wanted to. Samir and I felt like every day we were sending him out into this world with a bull's-eye on his back. This made me angry, but anger without positive action isn't productive. I have always been the kind of person whose anger lights a fire in their soul; my anger causes me to look for proactive and educated solutions to problems. I always told myself that I can't change what people say, I can't change what people believe, I can't change what people do, but I can control how I react to this.

Samir and I spent a lot of time shedding tears and sharing our feelings about how scared and worried we were about JSS going to school and the kids not understanding him and, in turn, picking on him. What could we do? How could we help him? Would this continue throughout all his school years? The typical worries that parents have were a million times worse for us due to the reality that JSS often didn't even realize when someone was being mean to him or bullying him. There is a purity, innocence, contentment, and honesty to autism that some people in this world take advantage of and see as a weakness. Sending your child out into the world with this type of vulnerability was absolutely terrifying.

Our first step was to put him in karate. The therapies we were doing to help him with his speech, socialization, and sensory regulation were very important, but we also knew that people didn't always use words to put others down or challenge them. It was now time for JSS to become physically and mentally strong, be ready to defend himself, and increase his self-confidence and self-esteem. Similar to how my mom had registered me in Tae Kwon Do to learn to defend myself as a woman and a visible minority, we wanted our son to be able to stand up for himself and be confident, strong, and powerful. We would do anything in our power to make sure he had every opportunity to live the life that he deserved to live with self-respect and dignity. I was worried about whether he would understand the instructions in the karate class, as often, they are given very quickly and in another language, but Samir had the solution: he would also join the class with JSS. Off they went to tackle another challenge.

As the days went on and we continued to face new and different challenges, my spiritual journey started evolving in a different direction. Now, when I thought about autism and our family, I found myself asking, "Why *not* me?" when I used to ask, "Why me?" I was now at a point where I was ready to stand on the mountaintop and yell, "My son has autism, and I'm proud of him and our family, and I wouldn't change anything about my life!" Actually going to a mountaintop and shouting these words may not have accomplished much, but this newfound acceptance gave me the confidence and strength to come up with some ideas for next steps. I was living a life that, at the time of JSS's birth, I knew nothing about, but now, I couldn't imagine my life without autism—and I didn't want to. I had come full circle.

JSS was now in grade 3, and he was continuing with intensive intervention at home with a multidisciplinary team of therapists through a specialized services contract. After much discussion, Samir and I decided it was time to tell JSS that he had autism. We wanted him to get the information and understanding about who he was from his loving parents and not the outside world, where some people have a habit of putting those down who think differently than the norm. We also wanted him to understand that he should be proud of himself, that having autism wasn't something he should be embarrassed about, and that it should never be seen as a negative defining factor in his life. We were proud of JSS, and we wanted him to be proud of himself too so he could go out into the world with complete confidence. He would always have our support, and we would always lift him up.

We asked JSS's behavioural therapist to create a booklet that would help JSS understand what autism is and why he had been diagnosed with autism. We continued using social stories, schedules, and explanations on paper; these are important for children with autism, as they set the rules down on paper and create a concrete sequence of events. It also gives them an opportunity to review the social story on their own as many times as they want and process the information over a period of time. Information can't just be explained once and then fully understood. JSS needed time to process the information to truly understand its impact or importance.

In creating this social story for JSS, we wanted him to understand that seeing the world differently and learning in a unique way wasn't a bad thing; in fact, it was refreshing and a much-needed quality in this world. He had his own strengths and gifts, and there was no way we were going to let him forget this due to the negativity or lack of understanding we often encounter in this world. We reviewed the booklet many times with JSS, and we knew that with his language delays, it would take time for him to process and understand what it meant. As his mother, I knew that JSS understood long before we read that booklet that he was different than the other kids; he just didn't see it as a problem or a cause for concern—and now, neither did we.

Once we had explained to JSS that he had been diagnosed with autism, our next step was to make autism a part of the vocabulary of the kids at school. It shouldn't be a secret or something that should have to be hidden because it was bad or negative. It wasn't just my job to teach JSS how to "live" in this world—it was also my job to raise awareness, wherever I could, about how JSS sees the world. I wanted people to realize that a simple kind gesture can set the foundation for any child to develop self-confidence. Those living with special needs require understanding, kindness, and patience. Autism is a part of many people's lives, and my goal became to raise awareness, increase acceptance, and ensure the final critical step of inclusion—plain and simple.

We spoke with JSS's teacher and received the support we needed to come into the class and speak to the kids about autism. Sometimes, I think we don't appreciate the openness and genuine goodness of children. The children in the class were interested, engaged, and asked questions. Autism became something children could speak about openly and not tuck away in a corner. We spoke about the challenges with language, socialization, routine, and self-regulation that many people with autism have to deal with every day. Children started speaking about other people in their lives who were facing similar challenges, and they began to understand and appreciate how tough and how long the days can be for JSS.

It normalized JSS's stimming, his repetitive questions, his self-talk, and the extra support he needed in order to participate in a game or activity at recess. They understood why an aide came into the class to help him. It wasn't because JSS wasn't smart; it was because he understood the world in a different way, and this was okay. They began to see JSS as their classmate and as their friend. We were building empathy and positive peer relations. The fact that he was different was no longer a burden or something that was funny. It was just JSS. Samir and I walked out of that room feeling victorious—and we were. We had a made an impact and positively changed the environment in JSS's class. I knew I gave him the correct name. He truly was the definition of victory.

After this first speech, the fire in my soul had grown, and I became even more passionate to spread autism awareness. I realized that as parents of a child with autism, it was our responsibility to educate and advocate for those living with special needs, thus ensuring these children aren't forgotten or left behind. My son had given us a very important job. I cared about every person who had autism, and my responsibility extended to all people living with autism and facing challenges similar to those faced by my son. It upset me to think that not everyone with autism necessarily had an advocate who could or would fight as passionately for them. Perhaps they faced challenges because English was their second language, or maybe they were living in impoverished circumstances, or maybe they lived in an abusive home environment. No matter what, I wouldn't let anyone be forgotten. Everyone has a right to be treated with dignity and respect and to have someone in their corner—and I decided I was going to be that someone. I knew I couldn't be everywhere and help everyone, but I also knew I had to start somewhere. I now knew, without any doubt, that my life's purpose was to help people with autism.

We continued with autism awareness speeches in JSS's class and soon started to speak not just to his class, but to his entire grade. We wanted to expand the scope of our reach. Our small presentation in grade 3 to a group of about twenty-five students expanded to over 120 students, which encompassed JSS's entire grade. In addition, we started to fine-tune our speeches—we prepared PowerPoint presentations in which we showed the kids simple videos that made autism easier to understand, and we began to distribute autism awareness bracelets and fidget spinners to the kids. Further, we began to go into the school for our autism speech in April. April is Autism Awareness Month, and April 2 is World Autism Awareness Day—the perfect time to share our autism story. This gave us an even greater opportunity to spread awareness about activities that were taking place around the world and in our city in order to promote autism. We did all this not only to raise awareness and to educate the students about autism, but to also keep the discussions going among the students.

I began to understand that sometimes, when people don't understand something, they fear it, avoid it, or make fun of it; however, when we "normalized" those living with autism, it opened up an entirely new understanding and acceptance among JSS's peers. Samir and I spoke openly and honestly to the kids and even asked the teachers to allow students to submit questions anonymously beforehand so we could answer them without generating any feelings of embarrassment. When we stood before the kids with confidence and acceptance, this translated into confidence in JSS and acceptance among his classmates. Many kids began to see that JSS was just like them. The same things made him happy, sad, and scared—he just expressed himself in a different way, and he needed more support in certain areas.

There was an analogy that always came to my mind before we would talk to the kids about autism: as parents, we teach our kids to look both ways before crossing the street for their safety and to eat their vegetables for their health. So too do we need to help them learn about accepting and including those living with special needs for the growth of their compassionate self. Growth as a human encompasses many aspects—compassion, in my opinion, being one of the greatest for the betterment of the human race. We often think in our quiet, non-famous lives that we can't make a difference, but that's not true. We can always make a tremendous difference. As we openly and honestly talk about our challenges and struggles, people start to view you as relatable, and this opens up a new door to understanding. We wanted to show the kids that they are part of a community, and we all have a responsibility to help each other within that community. Our expectation of responsibility and support didn't just extend to other people; it also extended to our own kids, who we've always taught to support and stand up for those who need them. It's a two-way street.

Our last speech in JSS's class was when he was in grade 6. Most of the kids had known JSS since kindergarten, and they would continue to go to school together until grade 9. It was important for us to speak to the students, but we realized it was also important for JSS to express how he felt. He was older now and could express himself more effectively than when he was only eight years old. Samir and I did a short presentation for the students, and then we gave the microphone to JSS. With his parents sitting on either side of him, he explained to his classmates how autism made him feel and the challenges he faced in his young life.

He had a voice, and he was using that voice to increase his confidence and self-acceptance. This was what I had always wanted, and it was exactly what we accomplished. I can't truly explain in words the pride and love I felt as I sat beside my son and listened to him advocate for himself. I could feel a powerful energy moving between me, Samir, and JSS. I knew we were all exactly where we were supposed to be. After his speech, I looked into his eyes and told him how proud I was of him, and how it took so much strength to stand in front of his peers and explain how difficult things can be for him at times. I told him he was an amazing son and young man. People all too often negatively define others by their diagnosis—today, if one was to define JSS's diagnosis, it would be defined by pure strength.

Things weren't perfect after these speeches. We still faced our challenges, as some kids forgot about our speeches or were negatively influenced by others, but there were always a few that remembered our presentations and tried to help JSS. Even though JSS continued to face some bullying, I always reminded him that for every kid that picked on him, he would find five others that support him. It was important for him to focus on the support he was receiving from his peers and to always stand up for himself.

I also taught both of my children to be nice to everyone unless someone gave you a reason not to be nice—then it's time to stand up for what is right. In addition to my self-confidence lessons, I would try and turn every negative situation into something positive. I remember JSS coming home one day and telling me that some of the boys at school called him a "nerd." I tried to explain to him that this was a good thing, as being called a nerd meant he was smart and did well in school. I told him that I was also a nerd in school, and this was a compliment, as I used my education and studies to do something positive in this world. He listened, but I knew he wasn't fully convinced. After a little research and a couple of calls, I sent JSS to school two days later with a T-shirt on that said "Nerd is Code for Genius." It goes without saying that he was never mocked again for being a nerd.

All these years, as we were teaching JSS to be proud of himself and to stand up for himself, we hadn't even realized the tremendous strength and power it was giving our little daughter, AKS. She had always been a very observant child and never missed a beat. Her brother's power, strength, advocacy, and determination were becoming a part of her personality, and this was helping her come into her own. Even as a baby, she was always very strong-willed and knew exactly what she wanted. I call her my little firecracker and my powerhouse. I didn't even notice when or how my little firecracker was following in our footsteps and becoming a powerful little advocate. There is so much truth in the saying that kids don't just learn from your words and what you tell them; in fact, they learn more from your actions and your examples. We were always very cautious in ensuring AKS was always included in everything, as we never wanted her to feel that she was second in line or being left behind. I didn't realize she was learning so much just by watching us.

I couldn't watch JSS all the time, but I had to find ways to see how he was socializing and ascertain where he was struggling. I remember taking AKS with me as we hid behind some trees near JSS's school, where we would observe him during recess, lunch, or outdoor physical education classes. We would watch to see how he was socializing and how the other kids were treating him. I would do this so I could later teach him about sarcasm, body language, and how some kids weren't really his friends and were making him do things so they could laugh "at him" and not laugh "with him." We also bought JSS a Fitbit watch in order for him to regulate his heart rate at school; however, I had a dual agenda. Each night, I would check the step counter on the watch. Although JSS loved to run, I had determined by watching him at school that some of the kids were telling him to chase them. They would run away from him and then laugh as he tried to catch up to the kids. He thought they were his friends—but they thought it was funny and entertaining. These subtleties were hard to explain to JSS as he approached his teenage years, and he didn't want to hear it; however, I wouldn't stop trying.

AKS was only about three or four years old when we would hide behind the trees at the school to watch JSS. AKS never ever complained about this, and she was always supportive. She saw it as our responsibility to protect

JSS, and she understood that in our family, no one fights alone. So there we were, me and my little sidekick—who, at such a tender age, would be asking me which boys were mean to Veer ji, or "older brother" in Punjabi. She would then take it upon herself to glare at those boys. She brought joy and laughter to me at a time when all I wanted to do was cry. "You can't do that to my brother," she would say powerfully, and I would chuckle and think, "Like mother, like daughter." She had zero tolerance for intolerance, just like her mom. She was an inspiration to me. From a young age, AKS understood the importance of equality and treating individuals fairly. To this day, her eyes still fill with tears whenever she thinks about someone picking on her brother or anyone with special needs.

It's a blessing for AKS to be able to express herself and understand language so naturally. Her strength in these areas has allowed her to always advocate for what she believes in articulately and confidently. Even when she was eighteen months old, people would meet her and be shocked at how much she had to say and how much she understood. Over time, I have come to realize that it's not just the spoken word that is her gift, but also the written word. However, her greatest gift is her desire to use her talents to help others.

At the age of five, she asked to be placed in a homeroom class with kids who had special needs so she could support them. As parents of a child with autism, we had taught JSS how to positively interact with others and understand this world; however, we had also equally taught our "neurotypical" daughter how to positively interact with children who have special needs and how to stand up for those who need a helping hand. We were witnessing the fruits of our labour. By the age of six, she was conducting speeches each year in her class about autism in order to raise awareness, acceptance, and inclusion, and she continues with this tradition every year during Autism Awareness Month. Most recently, she created a PowerPoint presentation for her grade 5 class with pictures of our family, a detailed explanation of what autism is, and how we can help those living with autism on a daily basis. I was so impressed by her confidence, intelligence, knowledge, and advocacy for her brother. I continue to tell her to this day that when I look at her report card, the first thing I check is her scores in the areas of exercising democratic rights and responsibilities within the learning community, her demonstration of respect and appreciation for diversity, whether she treats others with respect and compassion, and whether she makes responsible decisions. As one would expect, her teachers report exemplary strengths in these areas.

In addition to her autism awareness speeches, AKS also put up posters in her school to raise awareness about autism during Autism Awareness Month. I never imagined that the little seven-month-old baby who we brought to JSS's school, who sat with us as we listened to his diagnosis of autism, would one day stand up and advocate for her brother and for autism as a student in that same school. She had the same fire in her soul as I did, and she was already positively influencing her world. My friend Margaret Davenport-Freed was right when she said, "She is a diamond amongst gems."

Remarkably, not only was she an advocate in her school, she was also an advocate in our home and would often hold me up when I felt weak. I remember her hugging me as I cried in my kitchen after a tough day with JSS. "Don't cry, Mommy," she said, "everything is going to be okay. Veer ji just thinks differently, and we need to be more patient and understanding."

I would smile amid my tears. We should have never feared that she would feel left behind—she was, in fact, a leader in our home. She was a gift from God.

CHAPTER 9

Awareness, Acceptance, Inclusion

---

*"You are living proof to those who said it can't be done
that it will, in fact be done,
But more importantly, you are living proof to yourself that you
can and will accomplish every dream that your heart desires.*

*May God continue to protect you,
and may your angels continue to guide you.
May you continue to believe in yourself, advocate for what is
right, and be there for others who need your support.*

*Never let anyone tell you that having autism
is a disability or that it limits you in any way.
Having autism is an ability to bring a welcomed innocence,
open-mindedness, and a unique perspective to a world that can
be very closed-minded and judgmental.*

*This is a very powerful gift, and there is a reason
God gave you this gift.
Words cannot express how proud of you we are, my child.
We love you!"*

Mandeep K. Atwal
June 18, 2021
(JSS's grade 9 graduation)

ALTHOUGH JSS WAS ADVANCING IN MANY AREAS, WE STILL faced our struggles and challenges. I always tried to understand JSS from my soul, but many times, I remember not understanding why he behaved in certain ways. Even though I tried to be sympathetic, supportive, and loving, I couldn't truly understand his anguish and pain, as I didn't have autism.

However, it always seemed that whenever I was struggling to understand and help my son, the universe handed me little gifts. One day, Samir mentioned to me that he came across a book entitled *The Reason I Jump* by Naoki Higashida. The book was written by a thirteen-year-old boy who was diagnosed with autism. Samir had barely finished his sentence before I was on the computer trying to get my hands on a copy. Each night, when the kids were in bed, I would read Naoki's book, and tears would stream down my face. As much as I thought I understood my son, it reinforced in my mind that *he* was the one living a life with autism and trying to fit into a world that he didn't understand and, in many ways, didn't understand him. This book opened up areas in my mind I had not tapped into previously. Naoki's honest and heartfelt explanation of how hard life is for children with autism gave me new insight into how JSS must feel every day. I was having an epiphany. Once I finished the book, I learned to be more patient, understanding, and reflective. I understood that I was still learning too and that I would be learning about autism for the rest of my life. I'm helping and supporting my son who has autism, but I can never truly understand how he feels, as I don't live with the challenges and internal struggles that he faces every day.

Even today, when I feel disconnected from JSS, I turn back to Naoki's book, and it reminds my soul to become grounded, focused, and connected to my son once again. When Naoki spoke of how bad he felt when he made things difficult for his parents, it broke my heart to think that JSS could feel the same way when I got frustrated with him after we had a tough day. It was as if JSS was speaking through Naoki and telling me all the things that he was feeling inside. I received the depth of knowledge I needed to become an even better mother to my son, and I learned how much JSS loved and respected me even though he couldn't always express this sentiment. Although it's not always evident in their behaviour, Naoki also taught me that kids with autism have such a deep understanding of themselves and how they make others feel. I have never met Naoki, but I am so proud of him for helping so many people by shedding light on a condition that so often even medical professionals have a hard time defining and understanding. For me and many others, Naoki's book became a guiding force in understanding autism from the perspective of a child who lives with it every day. It reinforced my belief that there is tremendous power, strength, determination, and resilience among individuals living with autism.

◆ ◆ ◆

Before we knew it, twelve years with JSS had gone by. In those years, Samir and I had taken JSS to numerous medical appointments, many therapists, and watched him participate in many activities. JSS's intensive intervention therapies at home ended when he was nine years old, and now, it was time for us to focus on applying and using all the skills that he acquired since the age of three. We kicked it into high gear, as we wanted JSS to have as many experiences as he could socializing and developing his skills in many different areas. We wanted to offer him many options and possibilities to grow and develop and essentially find his passion.

During different times in the year, we enrolled JSS in karate, soccer, horseback riding, swimming, skating, basketball, hockey, wrestling, and social skills programs. Additionally, we introduced him to many STEM programs, like an at-home math program three times a week, app development, robotics, gaming, and coding. We also took him to summer camps at the science centre, the zoo, sports centers, and local technological institutes. It wasn't always smooth sailing with these activities. Even though we prepared a short written summary about JSS for each activity and camp that explained his strengths and weaknesses and highlighted the fact that he didn't engage in aggressive behaviour, he was refused at some camps, kicked out of a couple, and merely tolerated at others. We were always willing to work with organizations to ensure our son was included, but once again, we saw the preconceived notions of individuals surface, and we were often told that they were unable to "handle" a child with autism. JSS functioned in school without constant one-on-one support, but once people heard the word "autism," we were frequently told that they couldn't accept him because they couldn't give him the one-to-one attention and/or support they thought he would need.

Thankfully, we didn't face challenges at every single program. JSS attended and participated in some that were excellent, and the people we met there were very inclusive and created a great learning environment for JSS. However, our other negative experiences opened up my eyes to the fact that individuals with special needs weren't at the forefront of the planning process in many areas of the community and that there weren't a lot of options for inclusive camps or community supports for those living with autism. It shocked me that children with autism were so easily overlooked or dismissed. I thought about how tough life would be for these children, especially as they grow up and become adults within our community. JSS was lucky that he had such supportive parents who could vigorously advocate for him and that we weren't living in destitute conditions with limited resources, but my mind kept turning to those who didn't have a support system or resources.

Every person with autism has the right to live a life of dignity, to be offered opportunities, and to have the chance to pursue their passions. I had many days where I would come home enraged that my son was being excluded, but after openly and loudly expressing my thoughts to Samir, I would calm down, and together, we would come up with ideas of what we would do next to help JSS. Stewing in my own anger and frustration wouldn't get me anywhere, and it definitely wouldn't help my son or others living with autism. I had faith that one day, I would be able to express my concerns in a productive and articulate manner, and that's exactly what I'm doing as I type these words. All my experiences and interactions became learning experiences. I vowed to always be a voice for autism, and I constantly reminded my children to learn from negative experiences and to flourish from the positive ones. I also continuously reminded myself that the time would come where I would be able to express my anger and disappointment at my son's rejection, but I knew I had to do it in a positive way so as to effect positive changes and not in a negative way where it could create more isolation and anger.

When I was feeling down, I always seemed to be blessed with some incredible experience that reminded me we were on the right track, and I would then once again feel uplifted and inspired. I remember taking JSS horseback riding and feeling very spiritually connected and balanced in that environment. I was hoping that it would also have the same effect on JSS. He was anxious getting on his horse, Kyebar, but this twenty-year-old horse was the kindest and calmest animal I had ever met. I felt that horseback riding would definitely calm JSS's anxiety and help him become more focused and perhaps even help with his ADHD. As I said before, I was willing to try anything to help JSS feel more relaxed. I have never really been around a lot of animals, but the first day JSS was riding Kyebar, I turned to this beautiful horse and whispered to him, "Thank you for helping my son." The next thing I knew, Kyebar was putting his head very close to mine. I was definitely freaking out a little bit, but his caregiver noticed, turned to me, and said, "I think he just wants to give you a hug." As I cautiously and gently rubbed Kyebar's head, I realized there was tremendous power, strength, and hope everywhere. I started to see the world like JSS—with more than just my five senses. I had always been a spiritual person, but my trust in the spiritual realm was opening up even more.

Another incredible moment I witnessed that is locked in my memory occurred during JSS's swimming lesson. I never learned how to swim—in fact, I'm terrified of jumping into a pool, even if it's shallow, or putting my head underwater. It's a running joke in our family, and I always affectionately remind my kids that they're in swimming lessons for the sole purpose of saving me if I ever start drowning during a family vacation. JSS started swimming lessons at the age of eight, and although I was scared for him, I knew that learning to swim was an important skill. I had also read that sometimes kids with autism and ADHD benefit from swimming because it burns a lot of energy and can be a very relaxing and therapeutic activity.

Every Sunday, Samir and I would get up early and take JSS and his sister for swimming lessons. We would watch him nervously and be filled with pride as we went week after week and watched JSS learn how to swim. Finally, one Sunday morning after many lessons and some repeated levels of swimming, Samir and I looked on as JSS swam from one end of the pool to the other. Tears streamed down my face. I felt victorious and exhilarated as I reflected on all the things we were told he might not be able to accomplish. I thought to myself, "I am a 'neurotypical' adult who, to this day, would panic like a baby if I was thrown into the water, and here I am, watching my son with autism accomplish something I was never able to do during the entire course of my life."

At one point, as I watched him twirl in the water like a little otter and swim with his face to the ceiling, I saw a huge smile on his face, and I felt my soul vibrate at a higher frequency. I felt the dense, heavy energy of this earthly dimension, with all its melancholy, lift away. All the long days, the heartache, and the sleepless nights disappeared in the blink of an eye as I watched JSS happy, free, and successful. It's hard to explain how moments like this put everything into perspective and make all our efforts worthwhile, but somehow, they just do. Today, when I hesitate to do something, my kids remind me that I can accomplish anything if I put my mind to it and that trying is the most important thing, not necessarily winning. I can't help but smile at them when they tell me this. It's as if I'm looking in the mirror—they have been listening to all my advice and guidance, and now, they're giving it back to me. What more could I ask for? Oh, and I also promised them that once they're older, I'll take swimming lessons. Let's see what happens.

Our focus wasn't only on extracurricular activities; supporting JSS academically also played a huge role in our lives. We would spend hours doing homework with JSS. Every evening was a balancing act between homework, extracurricular activities, and my household responsibilities. Once the kids would go to bed, I would stay up and read the novels JSS was reading in school so I could discuss them with him while we did homework. As a family, we would also watch the movies made for the books JSS was reading in school. JSS is a visual learner, as many kids with autism are, and this visual representation and repetition of the book in picture form helped him put all the concepts together so he could better understand the storyline, themes, and symbolism of the book. God bless Samir, who would somehow find movies from the 1960s and 1970s and have them delivered to our house.

In addition to these efforts, I would also search the internet for book suggestions that therapists had given me in order to help JSS understand sarcasm and slang. I knew that this was a must when I said to JSS one day that my head was killing me and he went off in a panic thinking I was going to die from my headache. Small comments and slang that other children so effortlessly understood had to be taught to JSS just like a history or math lesson.

I remember reading a book to him that contained common slang followed by an explanation of their meaning. As I explained the meaning of some of these sayings, JSS would listen and then laugh hysterically. Then he turned to me with his beautiful, innocent brown eyes and asked me, "Mom, why don't people just say what they mean?" This was a profound question for such a young child to ask, and it was one to which I didn't have an answer. I once again saw the amazing sincerity and innocence of children with autism. It was so refreshing to hear his perspective, and I thought about how people with autism make the world a much more honest and heartwarming place to live in.

I tried to come up with an answer, but in the end, I turned to him and said, "That's a great question, sweetie. I really don't know why people don't always say what they mean. Maybe they're scared or not sure how others will react." He accepted my answer with the same sweet, innocent aura with which he had asked me the question. It was a moment he probably wouldn't remember, but one that I wouldn't forget. That moment, once again, opened my eyes and my heart to those living with autism. My little boy was helping me grow in so many important ways, and he had no idea he was making such an impact on me. I thought about how important it was to have individuals with autism at the forefront of society rather than allowing them to be ignored and excluded without respect or acknowledgment.

As a side note, I remember having a good laugh when JSS was about five years old and I asked him a question as I was heading out to a family function for the first time in a long time. I never usually got dressed up, let alone had the time to apply makeup. Samir and I could never go together to any large function, as taking JSS to an environment like that would be too overwhelming and overstimulating, so we took turns representing our family at different events. As I headed out the door in full makeup, I asked JSS, "How does Mommy look?" to which he replied, "Mommy, you look like a monster." I guess the smoky eye look didn't impress him. I laughed and said, "Don't worry, sweetie, tomorrow, Mommy will look like Mommy again." His response had me laughing all the way to the event. I thought in my mind, "Note to self . . . teach JSS that saying *exactly* what you mean all the time isn't always a good idea."

Even though I was so busy in life and doing as much as I could for JSS, I still felt as if something was missing. I thought about how I spent all my time making sure my family had exactly what they needed, but I wasn't doing anything for myself or using my skills in any way. As a mother, you struggle with your own identity when you put everything into your kids, especially when you're raising a child with autism or other special needs. I knew many mothers felt this way as they navigated the journey of motherhood, but I knew that I needed to do something more. In many ways, I felt lost.

I decided to hire someone to care for AKS a couple of times a week when JSS was at school so I could have some alone time. We were blessed to find Nancy, who the kids affectionately called Aunty Nancy. She was sent as an angel from my mom at a time when I needed some extra help and support so I could do some soul searching. Aunty Nancy would come in the morning, two times a week, which gave me a couple of hours of alone time. At first, it started with excursions to the mall. It was so relaxing to go to the mall and not have to worry about a screaming baby in a stroller or analyze every aspect of the mall in order to ensure JSS wouldn't be overstimulated and feel upset or overwhelmed by all the lights, sounds, security alarms, and people.

For the first six months or so of my freedom, I wandered aimlessly and reflected on my life. I thought about my journey and how far we had come. I thought about when and how JSS would become independent and what his future would look like. I thought about my law school education and how some people had criticized my decision to stay home and raise my kids. I knew what I was doing for JSS was essential for his future and his success; however, sadness and doubts still crept into my thoughts as I reflected on my "wasted" education. I would watch other women my age walk with their mothers, who would be doting over their grandchildren, and I would tear up thinking about how much I missed my mom and how she never had the opportunity to even meet AKS or witness in the physical realm how far JSS had come in his life.

I've always been very reflective and spiritual in nature, so I continued to ask God for guidance. I was looking for more in my life, but I had no idea what this "more" entailed. My kids meant the world to me, and I knew I was playing a huge role in their development, but I wanted to do something more. I wanted to create some sort of platform or path of my own. And then, one morning in August 2016, as I roamed the mall seeking direction, the path became clear.

"Ask and you shall receive" are the words that resonate in my mind when I think of what happened that morning. The quiet of the mall was broken by a sudden screaming and yelling. A young boy, perhaps around ten years of age, was screaming and grabbing a woman who was with him. He was repeating the same phrase and pulling this lady's hair. The lady was trying to talk to him and calm him down. Security was called, and a small group of people had gathered. I was overwhelmed; tears filled my eyes as I realized this boy had autism. I later discovered that the lady he was with was his aide. The security personnel were doing their best to keep the child calm, but I knew that the small group that had gathered wasn't helping. I knew his anxiety would increase. No one likes people staring at them when they're going through a tough time.

Once the boy had calmed down a little, I carefully approached the aide and asked if there was anything I could do to help. She indicated that he wanted to feel a lady's scarf or bag, perhaps as a way to regulate the overwhelming sensory inputs, and when the aide had told him no, he reacted in a way she had never witnessed. I frantically searched my purse for a sensory toy or a picture of my kids—anything that would help the boy in any way. The aide told me that she was okay, that the boy had never reacted in this way, and that his mother had been called to pick him up. Tears filled my eyes, and a lump developed in my throat as I thought about JSS and all the other children who face these challenges and aren't understood. I could see the anguish and frustration in that boy's eyes, and it was as if I was looking in my son's. Every child with autism faces these times of pain, and all of them have the right to be understood, helped, and appreciated. I wanted to help. I wanted to be a voice for autism.

After the boy's mother picked him up, I approached the security personnel and told them that they managed the situation very well. I asked them if they receive any training in helping people with autism who may be in the mall and then find themselves in overwhelming situations. I didn't have all the answers, but I knew I wanted to help in some way. The security personnel indicated that they didn't receive any such training. I told him about JSS's autism diagnosis, and I asked if I could speak to his manager about perhaps providing the security team with some visual cue cards to help people with autism. He directed me to the security manager's office, and within five minutes, I was speaking with the manager and asking if I could provide these cards to him, at my expense, so security personnel would have some assistance or help in communicating with individuals who have autism. He agreed. Little did I know that this was just the beginning of my new journey.

I began volunteering with Autism Calgary in August 2016, and in November of that year, they supported me as I stood in front of the security personnel of that very mall, conducting a presentation on how they can assist people living with autism. I explained a little bit about autism, how and why people with autism react in the way that they do, and what strategies can be applied in order to de-escalate situations and help those living with autism. My passion to raise awareness and understanding about autism and the importance of including those individuals living with autism allowed the words to just naturally flow out of my mouth. I was speaking from the heart and my personal experience. I had a desire to create my own platform and make a difference, and this was exactly what I was doing.

This first presentation turned into many other presentations. I presented at other malls, community associations, schools, childcare facilities, and even the local Calgary office of a major software company. I still had all of my obligations at home, but once the kids would go to bed, I would work on my presentations, perfecting them and ensuring that I included all the relevant information. That warm day in August had completely changed the direction of my life; I went from a wandering mother trying to find her path in life to a passionate public advocate spreading autism awareness within her community. I had come a long way from that heartbroken mother who would sit by her child's bed praying for him to "outgrow" his autism. I was exactly where I needed to be and doing exactly what I needed to do.

My advocacy expanded when I watched my son struggle with social interactions at school. I always taught JSS that it was better to be true to yourself and stand alone than to be with a group of people who didn't respect you or accept you for who you are. However, no one likes to be excluded or feel like an outsider, so I started a group at my son's school called Awareness, Acceptance, and Inclusion. The mandate of my group was to help those children at JSS's school who received a medical diagnosis that affected the way they learned, communicated, and socialized to feel accepted and included. The purpose of the group was to raise awareness and promote acceptance of people who think, learn, and socialize differently; to foster positive social and peer interactions at school; to help students feel accepted, included, and supported in spite of any challenges they may face due to their diagnosis; and to ensure that these students felt they were a part of the school.

I held monthly meetings with other moms who were facing similar challenges with their children, and I encouraged our children to get to know each other and become friends. I put up a monthly bulletin board in the school in order to encourage kindness, empathy, and compassion, and every April, during Autism Awareness Month, the board was dedicated to raising awareness about autism. I implemented a lunchtime program where parents could reach out to lunchroom supervisors to ensure their children were being included during the lunch hour and not facing any bullying. In addition, each morning during announcements, I would provide the school with a quote of the week. Each week, I would pick a quote that reinforced and built upon Dr. Temple Grandin's inspirational words: just because someone is different, they aren't less. I was tired but inspired.

I still faced challenges and problems along the way, as my group didn't have a huge following. Soon, it petered out to just me. However, I knew that I would never give up and that my son had given me a very important job. I realized that even if Samir and I had to work alone, as parents of a child with autism, it was our responsibility to educate and advocate for those living with special needs, thus ensuring that these children weren't forgotten or left behind. I found healing in helping. This healing continued when in December 2017, I received an award from Autism Calgary for my volunteer work giving speeches in the community about autism and increasing awareness and understanding. I felt like I had won the Noble Peace Prize, not because I had received public recognition, but because this was a huge milestone for our family in our journey of strength, resilience, courage, advocacy, and most importantly, acceptance. We were making a positive difference in our son's life and in the lives of others living with and trying to understand autism.

In 2018, while attending World Autism Awareness Day, I was briefly interviewed by CTV News about our autism journey, and our family was on television. This reinforced to JSS that he should be proud of who he is and that he should show the world that he is entitled to the same privileges and inclusion offered automatically to so many others. His face on the local news as a child with autism demonstrated not only his resiliency, but also how important it is to eliminate the stigma that is all too often automatically associated with a diagnosis of autism. Standing together as a community on World Autism Awareness Day is very important, as it brings autism into the limelight and to the forefront of conversations in many different settings. This is a necessary and all-important first step in the awareness, acceptance, and ultimately full inclusion of those living with autism. That evening, as we watched the news, we told JSS that he stood as an example to others of how important it is not to judge someone with a diagnosis of autism. We told him that we were very proud of him because he was brave enough to be himself and share with his community and his city that he had autism, and he was proud of it.

The more our passion grew, the more doors would open up for us. Writing has always been very therapeutic for me, and after a chance meeting with the publisher of our local community newsletter, I was given the opportunity to write an article. I wrote "Amazing Autism," which was published in the newsletter in April 2020—by a fortunate stroke of serendipity, it was during Autism Awareness Month, the perfect time to publish my article. I hoped that with this type of community exposure, families who were raising children on the autism spectrum would feel more comfortable sharing their experiences with each other, and we could build a strong autism community. I wanted families to know they weren't alone, and that the same fears, worries, and challenges they were facing were also a part of our daily lives. Many people approached me and spoke with me after the article was published and shared some very personal experiences. I was honoured and humbled. My soul was becoming more powerful by helping others—perhaps this was because my soul was growing in the exact direction that it was supposed to. I was fulfilling my soul's purpose.

CHAPTER 10
The Struggle is Real

———

*"I have watched my son, over the last fourteen years,
face and overcome challenges,
be excluded and be accepted,
struggle to succeed, and then achieve things
I could never achieve.*

*While all of these steps have made me so proud to be his mom,
one of the greatest moments for me was to hear him say that
he wants to start a new chapter in his life
where he helps people with autism.*

*I looked at this young soul in awe.
Someone who has gone through the challenges that he has gone
through would be completely justified in saying,
'I need to continue to help myself succeed.'*

*Instead, he wants to help others who are
facing challenges similar to his.
Thank you, JSS, for being my teacher.
You will help others with autism, and I will be
right there beside you.*

God bless you."

Mandeep K. Atwal
Feb 28, 2021

WITH ALL OUR EFFORTS AND CHALLENGES OVER THE PAST
decade or so, there were days when I felt completely mentally and physically depleted, but there was always a drive in me that helped me find the strength to go on. JSS was still receiving therapies at school from a speech language pathologist and an occupational therapist. We were blessed to find an amazing psychologist, Barbara Patterson, in 2015—she was a blessing from God and JSS's angels. JSS easily opened up to her, and we were so thankful for her strategies and honest and loving approach to helping children with autism. She had a passion for her job that we respected tremendously, and to this day, she helps our family deal with many issues that come up when raising a child on the spectrum.

We still weren't happy that JSS had to take medication for his ADHD and that he still had facial tics from the medication, so we tried everything we could to help him relax and focus. Everywhere I went, I opened my eyes and ears to look for ways to help JSS. We took him to a neurologist at the children's hospital to get more information on the tics and to make sure that it was, in fact, the medication that was causing these issues and not a different medical problem we had overlooked.

After doing more research on ADHD and homeopathic remedies, I started to rub essential oils on different parts of JSS's head and feet in the hopes that he would relax when he was supposed to and, conversely, stimulate or activate other parts of his brain when he required. In my research, I also learned that the brain is always developing new neural pathways, especially in children, and I was prepared to try whatever I could in order to help JSS in any way possible. We weren't doctors, but we treated and diagnosed JSS from the soul. I always believed the answers to medical issues lay somewhere between strict scientific remedies and the Eastern philosophies of treatment.

Eventually, through my constant research and conversations with medical professionals and other moms, we found ourselves driving around the city to biofeedback therapy, cranial sacral therapy, chiropractic therapy, auditory processing testing, a psychiatrist, yoga, and consultations with a clinic at the children's hospital in order to inquire about a novel neurometabolic diet which could potentially help children on the autism spectrum. I was in a desperate search to help JSS in any way I could. I wanted to increase his ability to focus, decrease his concentration challenges, support him through his daily transitions, and help make his frustrations easier to manage. I was also adamant to find a way to stop his ADHD mediation. Not everything I tried necessarily worked or stuck, but you never know unless you try. Needless to say, the struggle was real.

We also attended many community programs that were offered. Some were free and some were not, so we also had to watch our expenses closely, as we were a one-income family. Samir was always very mindful of saving for the kids while also ensuring they weren't denied any opportunity. This was a fine and difficult balance, but he always seemed to manage it seamlessly. We attended workshops and programs about ADHD, mind balance, managing life with a child with autism, speech language pathology, occupational therapy, and anything else that would help us succeed in raising JSS. At the time, we thought all the programs we were pursuing were helping us better raise JSS; however, over time, we realized all these avenues were also helping us grow and learn as parents and as humans.

Extracurricular activities and homework took up a tremendous amount of our time, and we were always cognizant of the fact that AKS also needed our attention. We never wanted her to feel left out or left behind, so we did everything in our power to ensure we gave her the same opportunities as JSS. We had read many books and spoken to many people about the impact that raising a special needs child can have on his or her sibling(s). We read about siblings becoming resentful and isolating themselves, as they felt neglected in the family. We harboured these fears when AKS was a baby, but as she developed and blossomed into a beautiful little girl, we realized that she was an equal partner in our family. In our family, we always made it clear that nobody fights alone, and each individual member of our family has different needs and requires different levels of support at different times. We taught our kids that we never compare our challenges or successes, we never compete with each other, and we always treat each other with love and respect. We reinforced the principle that we stand united with love and dedication for each other. As a sister and a daughter, AKS has always fulfilled her responsibilities in such a mature and passionate way. Her energy and aura amazes us and fills us with strength.

In addition to meeting JSS's every need, we also enrolled AKS in many activities and participated in her many school events. Samir had always volunteered for JSS's school field trips to ensure he had the support that he needed, so it was only fair that AKS received this same support. Off Samir went on school field trips, supporting his little girl. AKS was very active, and over the years she pursued, and continues to pursue, multiple activities—piano, dance, soccer, singing, drama, karate, swimming, in-line skating, ice skating, public speaking, and a variety of summer camps. She was also a social butterfly, and her many playdates and involvement in school groups kept us very busy.

Understanding social nuances, making friends, and appropriate social behaviour came very naturally to AKS, and this was a marked departure from the experiences and struggles we had faced with JSS. We were bewildered by the ease with which AKS would insert herself into social situations. We were delighted with her outgoing nature and ability to fit into many new situations; however, at the same time, our heart broke for JSS, who wanted to make friends so badly but just didn't know how to go about doing this in a socially acceptable manner. As loving parents, it was difficult to feel soul-resonating joy in the successes and accomplishments of one child when our other child was struggling so much in those same areas. As Samir so eloquently put it once, parents can only be as happy as their least happy child.

I clearly recall a very difficult Thursday night after parent-teacher interviews. JSS's teachers had informed us of the challenges he was facing in school trying to fit in with the other kids and the socially inappropriate questions and comments he was making at school. I found JSS quietly sobbing on our couch. I sat beside him and rubbed his head and asked him what was wrong. He said to me, "I want friends." I felt my heart drop and my soul ache. All of the feelings I had when he was three years old, all those fears about the world judging him and not accepting him, came rushing back to me. Even with all the education and awareness we were raising in the school about autism, I still knew friendships couldn't be forced. Some of the kids tried to include JSS whenever possible, but this still didn't result in the out-of-school social interactions and friendships JSS desired.

I knew we had done our best; however, it still didn't feel like enough. We explained to JSS that friendships take time and that Samir and I developed many of our lifelong friendships when we were adults. I reinforced all the things I had taught him and all the things he had learned about social interactions and making friends. I told him not to get disheartened and reminded him that where there is darkness, there is light; where there is fear, there is hope. You are the light, and you are the hope. This light and hope would lead him to the friends that would accept him for who he was and would stick by him through thick and thin. I also emphasized that some of the people in our lives at the present time weren't going to be there for a lifetime. I knew I was giving him the confidence and support that he needed to succeed; however, as a parent, this conversation kept me up for months at night, thinking, crying, and praying.

In addition to all the day-to-day hustle and bustle, JSS's medical challenges were also an ongoing concern. We continued to face JSS's previous medical challenges, but new issues also crept into the mix. We discovered after a trip to the zoo and a peanut-covered ice cream cone that JSS had a severe peanut and tree nut allergy and would have to carry an EpiPen for the rest of his life. This was very scary for us, as I knew I couldn't be with him all the time, and the thought of him having an anaphylactic attack and not being able to administer his own EpiPen is what a parent's nightmares are made of. I did the best I could. I put EpiPens everywhere you can imagine, I learned how to administer the EpiPen, we taught JSS how to use it, and I said a prayer every time he left the house without me. This silent prayer wasn't anything new; I had been doing this his entire life. We have had to administer the EpiPen to him once in his life, and that was one time too many. It was one of the scariest moments of our lives.

Whenever we felt a little bit of hopelessness and helplessness inch into our thoughts, without fail, God would send us some inspiration and hope. We were given the opportunity to hear Dr. Temple Grandin speak in February 2017, and to say she's one of the most inspirational people I have ever met is a huge understatement. Dr. Grandin is an international autism spokesperson and role model—she earned a bachelor's degree in psychology, followed by both a master's degree and a PhD in animal sciences. She has written many books and papers on both autism and animal sciences and is a leader in both these fields. She stated that she understood the reactions of animals to sensory stimuli because she has similar reactions to loud noises and sudden movements. In addition, she has spoken all over the world; she used her diagnosis of autism to change the world and to teach us that underestimating the talents and strengths of those living with autism would be a huge mistake.

I listened carefully as she explained how difficult her upbringing was and how hard school life and day-to-day life was for her. As she spoke, I saw my son in her, along with all the other individuals living with autism. To think of those that live in a world where they are misunderstood, mocked, and overloaded with sensory information, and where they are not able to express or explain to people how they feel or how they understand the world, brought tears to my eyes. Dr. Grandin reinforced how brave and resilient my son was to get up every day and live in a world that often didn't understand him or accept him for who he was as a human.

I had the opportunity to speak with Dr. Grandin briefly after her speech. I told her about JSS, and she reinforced the importance of having him involved in many activities, putting him in new situations, and helping him pursue his strengths, interests, and talents—as she kept telling the audience, "You need to bust them out of their siloes!" I left the building that night with a renewed sense of strength. When I got home, I quietly tiptoed into JSS's room as he slept, and I kissed his forehead, rubbed his head, and promised him that he would have every opportunity to become who he was meant to become in this life. Nothing was going to stop us, and no one was going to put us down. Challenges were inevitable, as Dr. Grandin had taught me, but by listening to her, I realized that dreams are only limited by the limits we place on them. I vowed that in our house, dreams would be limitless.

CHAPTER 11
The "Real World"

"Let me become who I am meant to be,
Let me be where I am meant to be."

Mandeep K. Atwal
May 1, 2023

THE YEARS KEPT FLYING BY, AND BEFORE WE KNEW IT, IT WAS
2019, and JSS started grade 8. He only had two more years left in middle
school, and then he would have to go to another school for grades 10,
11, and 12, which constituted high school in our district. We were very
anxious about where JSS would go to high school because this was going to
be a huge transition for him. We immediately started looking into private
special education high schools, as we knew that attending a public high
school with over two thousand students from grades 10 to 12 wasn't an
environment that would set JSS up for success. Being very familiar with
Individualized Program Plans (IPPs), in-depth parent-teacher interviews,
and meetings with the complex needs strategist at school, we knew exactly
what type of environment JSS needed in order to thrive.

We met a lot of wonderfully supportive people in the public school
system up until then; however, with the larger class sizes in high school,
the cuts to educational assistant hours, and the ever-decreasing government funding, we knew that many schools were struggling and that the
educational system wasn't set up for those with special needs. The sad
reality was, if you didn't function like a "neurotypical" child, you would

have to take your chances as a special needs child going to a public high school. This was by no means the fault of individual schools or school staff—as I mentioned earlier, we had been supported by some of the best up until that time. Unfortunately, this was the reality of our province's educational system and the funding, or lack thereof, that was available to those with special needs. I must also mention that our advocacy and involvement in the type of support JSS received played an instrumental role in his academic success. A team effort is required between the school and the parents in order for a child to succeed in school. However, in a public high school, our advocacy for JSS would only take us so far, as there would be a dramatic decrease in the level of support available to JSS as he transitioned from middle school to high school.

We had also done some research on public "cluster" schools for high school. These were schools designed specifically for children on the autism spectrum. We weren't a big fan of these, as our philosophy had always been integration, not segregation of children on the spectrum. Further, we always wanted JSS to be exposed to a broad range of peers; peers with different cultural backgrounds, different socioeconomic backgrounds, different skill levels, and different interests and talents. This was very important to us, as we always taught our kids that every person in our lives teaches us something, whether good or bad, and this well-rounded experience helps us determine who we want to be.

We had witnessed over the years that JSS's greatest growth occurred in environments where he faced challenges and interacted with many different people. This forced him to deal with many different social situations—whether positive or negative. Our goal was to expose JSS to the "real world" and help him understand that some people will accept him, and some will not; some will help him, and some will not. Over the years, we felt that JSS's exposure to many different scenarios helped build his confidence and made him even more resilient. This confidence and resilience would prepare him to live as an independent adult. We were also mindful of the fact that we had to continue reminding JSS that although sometimes we have to deal with tough situations, often, when we least expect it, someone lends us a helping hand.

We had also heard that the academic support offered at cluster schools wasn't on par with a "typical" high school. I had an interesting conversation with a lady who worked in the educational system in Australia, and she told me they didn't believe in segregated classes. Kids with autism, regardless of the severity, were integrated into the school. If they needed extra support, they were provided with it, but they were still a part of the "regular" stream. They were never separated; thus, the importance and value of those living with autism in the community was reinforced. I admired and respected this type of system of inclusion and acceptance and was saddened that it didn't exist here.

The point of the cluster schools quickly became moot, as even these schools were being eliminated due to funding cuts. The other public high school options didn't fit with JSS at all. There were schools for children with extreme behavioural concerns or children who faced a lot of cognitive or academic challenges. We felt like there was no place for JSS to go. He didn't face severe academic delays, and he didn't suffer from any aggressive behaviours or tendencies. This was never a concern as we navigated our autism journey. He had been attending the "regular" school stream since preschool. He was integrated. So where would kids like JSS go? They fell in the middle of the spectrum of support—they didn't require one-on-one, hands-on support, but they also couldn't be left on their own with no support.

We were blessed to have the funds to pay the tuition that was required to enroll in a special education private school, so we continued researching. During the fall of 2019, after many hours of reading, we were interested in three private schools that helped students with diagnosed learning disabilities.

The first school we looked into was Rundle Academy, which was a private school that also received an Alberta Education Grant from the provincial government.[6] Rundle Academy stated on its website:

---

6   Curtis Riep, *Private Schools Funding in Alberta: Scaling-Up Privatization*, Public School Boards' Association of Alberta, April 2022, https://public-schools.ab.ca/wp-content/uploads/2022/05/Private-Schools-Funding-in-Alberta.pdf.

> We do not offer a program or have support for students
> who apply with a diagnosis on the Autism spectrum.[7]

We were shocked to read such a broad and all-encompassing statement on their website. There was no opportunity for JSS to even be considered for a placement in this school. We were learning a lot about how autism "fit" or "didn't fit" into our society. We quickly moved on to the other two schools, as Rundle Academy wasn't even going to look at our son. Although the thought of so many children being overlooked on the basis of their diagnosis alone filled me with frustration and anger, we had to use our energy to help JSS find the best place for his future. A school that didn't even consider a child on the spectrum was definitely not the place for our son.

It's interesting to note that in the process of writing this book, I looked at the Rundle Academy website again and saw that they have since created a "studio" program that began in the fall of 2021 for grades 7, 8, and 9, where they accept applications from children on the autism spectrum; however, this is an online program only. The statement on their website indicating that they do not accept children with autism for in-person classes is still there as of spring 2023. Once again, this didn't sit well with me, as our entire philosophy is integration, not segregation, of those living with autism. I understand that many children, with or without a diagnosis of autism, prefer online learning, but the presumption should not be made that this type of programming is the only suitable option for children with autism.

Determining appropriate methods of schooling should be done on a case-by-case basis, including actually meeting the child. Each child with autism is different and has different needs, and as we say in the autism community, "If you know one person with autism . . . you know one person with autism." We are all different people, and we all learn in different ways; children with autism shouldn't be grouped into one category where they aren't afforded the same opportunity to pursue in-person schooling as children without autism. JSS is an extremely social child, and he has

---

7   "Academy Admissions," Rundle Academy, accessed July 13, 2022, https://rundle.ab.ca/academy/academy-admissions/).

learned so many life skills in the classroom. He loves going to school. Why should he, or any other child with autism, be limited to an online learning option? A couple of years later, during the COVID-19 pandemic, we would find that JSS hated online learning, and he longed to go back to school. We would see the impact of online learning in the greater community on many children as they were forced to isolate and not be a part of their school community. This type of isolation and exclusion is something that children with autism face on an ongoing basis, and this should be seen as a community problem that needs to be rectified.

But right now, with Rundle Academy not even being an option, we looked into two other private schools in Calgary that focused their support on students with diagnosed learning disabilities: Foothills Academy and Calgary Academy. There was no indication on either of their websites that they automatically refused children on the autism spectrum, so we thought that they would be a better match for JSS, as they would accept him for who he is and could meet his needs. This also gave us some reassurance that they would see the ability and power in JSS to become a successful member of society. We were encouraged to find that they didn't appear to fall victim to the preconceived notions about autism that many organizations hold, and we thought that one of these schools would be the place for our son—a place of acceptance and support.

Our first application went to Foothills Academy. Foothills Academy is a designated special education private school (DSEPS) for students in grades 3 to 12 who have diagnosed learning disabilities. We learned that "designated special education private schools are funded private schools that have been given special approval and funding by the Minister of Education, where the sole purpose of the school is to serve students who are identified with a mild, moderate or severe disability."[8] We were impressed by their mission statement and philosophy. Foothills Academy's mission statement is:

> . . . to facilitate learning in persons, primarily youth and children, identified as having a Learning Disability by providing quality educational programs and a supportive

8   "Private Schools," Alberta.ca, https://www.alberta.ca/private-schools.aspx.

environment for families and staff. We recognize that we are interdependent with our global community – by participating in research, public education, in-service and advocacy, through community service.[9]

Foothills Academy's philosophy:

> . . . was built around the belief that all students with Learning Disabilities have exceptional potential, and with the right supports and guidance, they can achieve great success in school, post-secondary, and the workplace. We understand the difficulties and challenges facing students and their families, be it academic, social, emotional/behavioural, or financial.[10]

We were impressed with their mission statement, their philosophy, and their three core values: find understanding, build confidence, and maximize potential.[11] In JSS's psychological educational assessment, he had been diagnosed with a learning disability in oral language—in particular, he had challenges with expressive language. Foothills Academy listed the following criteria in their application process:

1. The child **must have a primary diagnosis of a** Learning Disability (stated in a psycho-educational assessment completed in the past 2 years).
2. The child must have average to above-average intelligence.
3. We are **unable** to accept students with severe social/emotional/behavioural needs or those requiring 1:1 classroom support in order to be successful.[12]

9   "Mission & Philosophy," Foothills Academy, accessed July 13, 2022, https://www.foothillsacademy.org/about-foothills/mission-philosophy.
10 "Mission & Philosophy," Foothills Academy, accessed July 13, 2022.
11 "Mission & Philosophy," Foothills Academy, accessed July 13, 2022.
12 "School Admission Criteria," Foothills Academy, accessed July 13, 2022, https://www.foothillsacademy.org/our-school/admissions/criteria.

They go on to define a learning disability as the following:

> Learning Disabilities range in severity and may inter-
> fere with the acquisition and use of one or more of
> the following:
>
> - oral language (e.g. listening, speaking, understanding);
> - reading (e.g. decoding, phonetic knowledge, word recogni-
>   tion, comprehension);
> - written language (e.g. spelling and written expression); and
> - mathematics (e.g. computation, problem solving).[13]

We were also impressed by the fact that they had an occupational therapist and speech language pathologist on hand. Their roles were described
as follows:

> These services focus upon supporting students with strat-
> egies for regulation, executive functioning, practical and
> functional language and developing engaging and sup-
> portive classroom environments. Although the services
> are predominantly found in the younger years of Teams
> 1 and 2, high-school students also receive the services
> when necessary.[14]

After reading all these requirements, we felt reassured in applying to
Foothills Academy, as these were JSS's main challenges. It seemed like the
perfect match. We submitted JSS's application in September 2019, including the up-to-date psychological educational assessment indicating that
JSS's primary learning challenge was his learning disability in oral language. In the testing that was done in July 2019, he scored in the average
range except for verbal IQ (where he was borderline) and knowledge
(where he had a mild delay). His psychologist, Barbara, indicated that his
results should be interpreted cautiously, and as we had explained, these

---

13 "About Learning Disabilities," Foothills Academy, accessed July 13, 2022, https://
    www.foothillsacademy.org/about-foothills/about-learning-disabilities.
14 "OT and SLP," Foothills Academy, accessed July 13, 2022, https://www.
    foothillsacademy.org/our-school/explore-our-school/student-support/ot-slp.

results reflected his learning disability and not his IQ. We knew that this point would become clear once they met with JSS. Further, we provided all the necessary documentation indicating that JSS had been in the "regular" school stream since kindergarten, that he had successfully completed the curriculum each year, and that he didn't have any severe social, emotional, or behavioural problems. We also booked a tour for November 2019.

On October 4, 2019, we received the following email:

> Unfortunately, based on the documents we have received, the intake committee has reached the decision that the programming at Foothills Academy will not be a suitable fit for JSS's needs. We loved to see the many positive assets JSS has as a student and an individual. However, although we have carefully designed a program for children with a primary diagnosis of a Learning Disability and average IQ (minimum FSIQ = 85), our expertise does not lie outside of this profile. Unfortunately, we aren't equipped to adequately support students with diagnoses of expressive and receptive language delays, or with significant needs related to ASD.

I was stunned. This decision was made without even meeting JSS. I was bewildered, especially in light of the fact that their website clearly indicated that they helped kids with learning disabilities in oral language, including listening, speaking, and understanding. How could they possibly say they couldn't adequately support kids with expressive and receptive language delays?

Furthermore, Barbara had indicated in JSS's psychological educational assessment that when one meets him, it becomes apparent that he *does not* present with significant delays related to autism, and that the academic challenges he faces are related to his learning disability, not his ability to perform academically. Why was Foothills Academy saying they couldn't support those with significant needs related to ASD when the psychological educational assessment they asked for explained that the opposite was true for JSS? This didn't make any sense to me. We responded to the email asking them to meet with JSS. We emphasized that what was written on paper about JSS wasn't a true reflection of who he is or his capabilities, and as his psychologist had indicated in the psychological educational assessment, he doesn't present with significant delays related to autism, and that the academic challenges he faces are related to his learning disability, not his ability to perform academically. We also reinforced that since the age of three, JSS had been integrated into the "regular" or "traditional" school system, had been functioning in class without constant one-on-one support, and didn't require modification of the curriculum. He only required smaller class sizes and innovative techniques when it came to learning the curriculum. He was a hands-on and visual learner.

Still, Foothills Academy refused to meet JSS, indicating once again that their program was "not designed to support students with receptive and expressive language delays." They further indicated that they believed he would "struggle greatly" within their program, which relies heavily on verbal comprehension skills. In our view, it was apparent that the decision not to accept JSS was made once the application contained the term "autism spectrum disorder." It didn't matter how capable he was, how he had kept up with the school curriculum for nine years, how many extra-curricular activities he was involved in, or how he would be a positive member of the Foothills community—in our eyes, it was obvious that the only thing that mattered to the school was his autism diagnosis. The words in their mission statement and philosophy whirled around in my head: "potential, support, guidance, achieve." We felt that our greatest fear when JSS was a child had just been realized—he was being defined and judged on the basis of his diagnosis alone.

I thought to myself, "Was it not the entire purpose of a designated special education school to support those with special needs? Wasn't this why they were getting funding from the government?" For his entire life, JSS was told he had special needs and needed support—why was he being told now that he had the wrong type of special need? The fact that Foothills Academy didn't even give JSS the opportunity to meet with them in-person left us dejected and disappointed and reinforced in our mind that our fight for JSS was going to be a long one. Individuals on the spectrum were already living in a world that didn't understand them, and now the very institutions that were designed to help them, and to which we were turning to for help, were also rejecting these kids without even meeting them. When we told JSS the decision that Foothills Academy had made, tears streamed down his face, and he asked us, "Did they reject me because I have autism? If I didn't have autism, would I have been accepted?" As I held back my tears, I said to him that it didn't matter what decision they would have made if he didn't have autism. The only thing I did know was that Foothills Academy wasn't the right fit, not because they didn't accept him, but because we no longer respected or accepted them. We didn't pursue Foothills Academy any further.

We turned our attention next to Calgary Academy. This was another private school that received an Alberta Education Grant from the provincial government.[15] Their focus was helping children with diagnosed learning disabilities. In their mission statement, they write:

> We design engaging, dynamic, student-centered experiences that nurture a caring, inclusive culture and instill a love of learning.[16]

Their vision is:

> To be a beacon of possibility for richly personalized, engaging learning experiences that empower learners to pursue lives of passion and purpose.[17]

Samir and I attended a parent tour of the school in November 2019, and we were impressed by the school's focus on developing a child-centered plan for learning, the small class sizes, the importance placed on increasing the confidence of the student, the goal of helping students to become contributing members of society, and the community service element. The school focused on inclusive education and encouraged students to achieve their full potential with confidence. The other aspect of Calgary Academy that we really liked was that their speciality was in remediating learning difficulties. In other words, their primary focus was to understand the root

---

15 "Private Schools," Alberta.ca.

16 "Mission," Calgary Academy, accessed July 13, 2022, https://calgaryacademy. com/ca-overview/.

17 "Vision," Calgary Academy, accessed July 13, 2022, https://calgaryacademy. com/ca-overview/.

cause of each child's learning difficulties and then focus on developing a customized learning plan to address the areas of need, using the child's natural strengths to boost their confidence in the learning experience. Students were taught personalized strategies that could be applied in many contexts, and this would ensure success based on each individual child's strengths. We wanted to provide JSS with the tools to learn in a way that worked for him while also taking into account his challenges with language. Once he had these tools, he would feel more confident in the way he was learning. We wanted him to become an empowered learner.

In July 2020, we submitted all the material required for JSS's application, and we were told that in October 2020, Calgary Academy would be in touch with us in order to set up a time to meet JSS. He was very excited to meet the staff at the school, and it seemed like his confidence was coming back after Foothills Academy had refused to even meet with him. I didn't realize at the time of the refusal how much it affected him, and would still affect him almost a year later. He would ask me if Foothills Academy would have met him if he didn't have autism, if they would have met his sister, AKS, who doesn't have autism, and if there was something wrong with him. He would sometimes say he wished he didn't have autism because he would have been treated better in this world.

This broke my heart, but I always told him that if I could go back in time, I wouldn't change one thing about our lives together—not only was he the most courageous and tenacious kid I knew, but he had changed the trajectory of my life for the better. He had given my soul a passion and a fire; he had created an advocate for a cause that was so important and so often overlooked. He had given me the honour of being his voice—but only for now, because I knew that one day, his voice would be a powerful and confident roar that would reach the ends of the earth. Samir and I always encouraged JSS to be true to himself and not let negative people and situations bring him down, but as a mother, when I would lay my head down on my pillow at night, his questions caused me to softly sob. There isn't a loving mother in the world who wants to see her child face rejection, heartache, judgment, or a loss of opportunities. However, every morning, I would leave those tears on my pillow because when a new day started, I knew it was another day to get to work and to fight for the rights of those living with autism.

On November 13, 2020, we received an email from Calgary Academy indicating that JSS didn't receive a spot at their school. Once again, this decision was made without meeting JSS or engaging in any discussion with him; the school hadn't followed up in October 2020 to set up a time to meet JSS, as they said they would. The refusal indicated the following:

> We appreciate your patience with us while we have been planning for the upcoming school year. We would like to let you know that the Admissions Committee puts a great deal of time and effort into examining all documentation contained within an application to determine if Calgary Academy would be able to provide an educational environment in which a student could achieve academic, social, and emotional success. Many factors are considered on both an individual level and the needs of the existing group of students in the corresponding grade. Before applicants are considered for our programs, they must meet our admittance criteria: average to above average intelligence and no history of social, emotional or behavioural issues that have required extra support.

> After an extensive discussion based on our current classroom groupings and the amount of support JSS may require, it is with deep regret that we inform you that we are unable to consider him for placement for the 2021-2022 school year. With the information gathered, we do not believe that we have the staff, services or supports to provide JSS with an appropriate program and successful school experience at Calgary Academy.

We were at a complete loss. JSS had been functioning in the "regular" stream for his entire school career; his psychologist, Barbara, had indicated that he didn't suffer from any social, emotional, or behavioural issues that caused him not to function successfully in class or school; and he had received less support in the public school system than he would receive in a private school, where their focus is to support children with diagnosed learning disabilities. He had, in fact, successfully completed nine years in that "less supportive" system. Further, in their own refusal, they say that according to their current classroom groupings, the amount of support JSS "may" require is not something that they can accommodate. But wouldn't it have been a good idea to at least meet with the child before making their final decision? Perhaps meeting and speaking with JSS to determine how much support he "may" require would have helped them make a decision based on all the relevant criteria. It's interesting that their "extensive discussion" about JSS and the support that he may need occurred without ever taking the time to meet with him or having a conversation with him. I further questioned why they didn't turn to his psychologist or current teachers before deciding how much support JSS might require and whether he would be a good fit for the school.

We were left with the impression that this was a form letter, and once again, we believed that JSS's diagnosis of autism was the reason for the rejection. I had discussions with many friends prior to and during our application process to Calgary Academy. I was informed of students who were accepted at Calgary Academy who suffered from anxiety, depression, and other mental health conditions, which, in my opinion, can be classified as "social, emotional or behavioural issues," as stated in Calgary Academy's rejection email. I was happy that students facing these challenges were accepted in the school and receiving the support that they needed, but what about kids with autism? Wasn't the entire premise of these schools to foster inclusion of those with special diagnosed learning needs and not exclusion? Where did we fit in? We were once again faced with the reality that JSS was being judged and pigeonholed on the basis of his diagnosis alone. The school had determined who he was, what supports he might require, and how he might behave all without even meeting with him or speaking with him.

With so many kids being diagnosed with autism in the last ten years, would it not be reasonable for me to assume that a private school that receives grants or funding from the government and emphasizes its focus on helping children with diagnosed learning disabilities would receive the training and resources they needed to support a child on the spectrum?

Institutions that claimed to help those with special needs were making decisions without even meeting their potential students, and perhaps even rejecting those who would and could benefit from the very services these institutions were designed to provide. I may not have all the answers, but I was and am ready to have these discussions.

I want to make it clear that I am in no way criticizing the ability of the teachers at these schools or the ability of these private education schools to support children with special needs. The importance of these schools is evident in the number of applications they receive and the number of children who require extra support. My critique is of the admissions process and the manner in which they deal with applications from children on the autism spectrum. I only bring these issues to light because without identifying the problems within our society and schools, we can't bring about positive changes to the status quo. If nobody says anything, nothing will change.

We didn't ask Calgary Academy to meet with our son. We wanted to show JSS that we don't beg people to accept us. We are proud of who we are, and we look for other positive ways to change the things in our society that aren't fair. We look for solutions and opportunities, and we never give up. Even still, these rejections bothered JSS; he kept asking why he had autism and why his life had to be this way. It was hard to hear this self-doubt, but there was no way I was going to let anyone or any institution decrease JSS's self-confidence, cause him to question himself, or undo all the progress he had made in his life. I have always been a very passionate person, and I continued to teach my kids the mantra that it's better to die with dignity than to live without self-respect. A little extreme, perhaps, but very accurate and a good life lesson.

I should note that as all of these events were transpiring, and as we were dealing with these rejections, AKS didn't quietly stand by and listen. Every day, she would ask me whether Veer ji's schools had made a decision, and when I gave her the answer, she got very fired up and would say, "Why are autism kids treated so differently?! Don't worry, Veer ji, we don't want them if they can't accept you! I am never going to let anyone with autism be treated unfairly!" I would quietly smile as she stomped around the house in disbelief. I knew all these life lessons were building confidence, strength, and power within our entire family, and this was something that no institution could deny us or take away from us.

Later in my life, I would deal with the issues raised by Foothills Academy's and Calgary Academy's decisions and let others know what we faced and how we felt. As a lawyer, I know that achieving justice, fairness, and equality in any situation isn't accomplished overnight, but is rather an ongoing process. We can achieve small noble victories by challenging current standards through public commentary. A noble victory doesn't always come easily. The change may not be a big splash in the water, but we have to remember that even a small ripple in the water can bring important issues to the front line and initiate change. As I sit here and type our story, I feel as if I'm bringing forth some very important issues and getting some justice for our son, who has every right to be afforded the same opportunities as other children. We need to break the barrier or stigma around autism, and this takes a community approach with schools, the government, families, and most importantly, those living with autism, all on board.

But that would come later. For now, time was ticking—it was December 2020, JSS would go into grade 10 in September 2021, and we still needed to find a place for him. We looked into one other public school, but after a lot of research and discussion with the school, we realized that with class sizes exceeding forty students, he wouldn't receive the support he needed in order to succeed. He had been attending the "regular" stream of schooling with a broader community of his peers, but now, it seemed there wasn't a spot for him there. The many years spent trying to integrate him into the community seemed futile, as the power of his successes didn't seem to stand up to the stigma attached to his autism diagnosis.

We turned our attention to New Heights School and Learning Services. This was a designated special education school, and they state the following about their programs:

> Our school programs are created for students who have
> autism spectrum disorder or similar learning differences
> such as sensory integration difficulties, impairments in

social interaction, and difficulties with emotional control and interpersonal skills.[18]

We spoke with the staff at the school to get a better understanding of the programming and support that would be available to JSS. We learned that JSS would follow the "regular" Alberta education curriculum with adaptations, not just modifications. We liked the other things the school offered: the class sizes were very small; numerous counsellors would be available to us, including a family counsellor; a transition to adulthood program (T2A) and an employment program would be accessible to JSS, and work experience would be a big part of his high school years; gaming and STEM courses were available; and even a driver's education program. Further, ongoing coaching for social and life skills at school was also a part of the daily curriculum. After collecting all the relevant information, we submitted our application for JSS in January 2021.

In March 2021, we toured the school. We met the high school teachers and had the opportunity to observe some of the students in the class. JSS was happy and excited to have a look at the school, but I could see the apprehension in his face as he feared another rejection. I realized then how delicate the psyche of a child can be and how facing rejection based on a diagnosis could cause children to question their self-worth and value. This can be even more overwhelming for a child on the spectrum who may have difficulty expressing themselves. We explained to JSS that New Heights was a school that welcomed students with autism and that his diagnosis wasn't something he had to hide or explain away. He could be who he was, and it was welcomed, celebrated, and accepted. We didn't have to fight to be included. We were seen. We were respected. I wished the whole world was like that for my son and all individuals on the autism spectrum, but I guess that's why I was given this soul journey—so I could initiate a positive change.

---

18 "Grades 1-12 School Program," New Heights School & Learning Services, accessed May 9, 2023, https://www.newheightscalgary.com/programs/school-aged/.

JSS was placed on a waitlist. This didn't surprise me, as by 2018, the number of children diagnosed with autism in Canada was one in sixty-six.[19] I'm sure New Heights received numerous applications for admission. Small class sizes were a definite asset; however, this also meant that there were limited spots available. We patiently waited and prayed.

In June 2021, a spot opened up at New Heights, and we accepted. We found a sense of peace once we made the decision to send JSS to New Heights. It was a peace that we longed for, and Samir and I also learned some important lessons along the way. We always tried to integrate and include JSS in our community, with other "typically" developing children, whether in school or extracurricular activities. JSS had always grown and flourished when he was exposed to many different types of environments and a broad group of peers with different abilities; however, as he got older, we found the options became more limited with respect to who would accept JSS. This definitely made us feel tremendous frustration and disappointment that those living with autism were being discriminated against in many different environments.

However, once JSS started attending New Heights, we realized this entire process was a lesson for our family and for our individual soul growth. We realized there's still a tremendous amount of work that needs to be done within many educational institutions in order to ensure inclusion of those on the autism spectrum, but we also realized that at New Heights, JSS was in a new environment, growing and learning in a new way. He was with a peer group who didn't judge him, he was free to be himself every day, and the teachers and staff had a compassionate touch and a level of understanding that was every parent's dream.

In addition, as part of his work experience at school, JSS started working at the Mustard Seed, a homeless shelter. Not only was he learning very important life skills, but he was also giving back to our community. Many times during our journey, people had stepped forward to help and support us, and now, he was doing the same for others who were facing

---

19 "Infographic: Autism Spectrum Disorder among Children and Youth in Canada," Government of Canada, last modified March 29, 2018, https://www.canada.ca/en/public-health/services/publications/diseases-conditions/infographic-autism-spectrum-disorder-children-youth-canada-2018.html.

very challenging situations. We have always taught JSS that just as we feel our community has a responsibility to help him, we also have a responsibility to help our community. This is what I often refer to as the positive ripple effect. You never know how your positive actions can turn into a positive world reaction. We are part of a world community, and at a soul level, we know that what we do to others is the outcome we are creating for ourselves. At New Heights, we also found camaraderie with other parents. Without any words, we understood that we were all coming from a similar place and had faced similar challenges, stereotypes, preconceived notions, and judgments from people and institutions. We found comfort and strength in familiarity and a lack of judgment.

Again, I'm not accepting or excusing the manner in which the schools that refused JSS dealt with his applications; rather, I choose to look at the situation as a way for my son to learn, to grow, and to become a valued, respected, and self-assured member of society. I know I'll never let JSS's dreams and goals of being included and accepted fall by the wayside. This is a fight I'll continue for the rest of my journey on this earth. I know that some people may be thinking, "See, JSS 'fits' into a school that specializes in helping kids with autism, so this is where he should be." My response is that this is not a judgment for them or anyone else to make.

Pigeonholing a child based purely on a diagnosis is not an effective way of including and accepting those living with special needs. If a family decides that a specialized school that supports children with autism is the best option for their family, then that is the right decision for them. However, institutions like special education private schools that are supposed to be helping those living in our society with special needs, especially children, shouldn't be making arbitrary decisions. In our case, we felt that predetermining JSS's specific abilities and skills based solely on paper, failing to consult with JSS's teachers, his parents, or his therapists on any level, and most importantly, failing to meet with him resulted in a capricious decision. Unfairly assuming that someone has limited skills based upon their diagnosis is a mentality based on stereotypes that needs to be eradicated from our society in order for us to advance.

Breaking free of these preconceived notions and barriers becomes nearly impossible if these notions and barriers aren't challenged or brought to the attention of the public. If we don't shed light on these issues, they will continue to exist within the intuitions that are shaping and educating our children. Opening up our thinking and taking the time to get to know those living with autism is the first step; nonjudgmental and openhearted inclusion is the necessary second step.

CHAPTER 12

Window of Opportunity

———

"Happy 15th Birthday to our dear son, JSS!

*Fifteen years have passed, and my heart
still sees you as my little boy.
But when I look at you with my soul, I see a young man
with a heart of gold.
I didn't know when I gave you your name that you would truly
be the 'Guardian of Victory.'*

*When you catch me looking at you in awe,
I am humbled by the lessons you have taught me
and how strong you truly are.
I will not deny that our journey has not been an easy one,
But the deep love, respect, admiration, and pride that I have
for you makes the difficult days fade away.*

*We love you more than you will ever know, and we want to
thank you for teaching us the meaning of unconditional love.*

*Happy Birthday to our precious child. May God bless you,
protect you, and give you everything you need. xo"*

Mandeep K. Atwal
May 12, 2021

WITHOUT A DOUBT, THE YEARS LEADING UP TO 2020 WERE taxing and demanding. The entire process of determining JSS's future schooling was a very stressful time for our family; however, it wasn't our only challenge in those years. At the same time, we were dealing with one of the biggest decisions of JSS's life. Our decision regarding this challenge could have a lifelong impact on JSS; it was a decision that would eventually come to fruition in a completely different country almost two years after we decided to walk down this path.

On August 3, 2018, I received an email from Insception Lifebank, Canada's largest and most accredited cord blood program. We had JSS's stem cells stored with them since his birth, and they sent me regular emails with respect to new therapies and scientific research being conducted with stem cells. The email I received on this day caught my attention—it offered us a novel option to help JSS only available in the United States. As you may recall in chapter 2, I had an overwhelming feeling before JSS's birth to collect and store his stem cells. Although we weren't able to collect the full amount of stem cells, as he was born with the cord around his neck and the safest option was to cut the cord, we were able to collect AKS's stem cells in full during her delivery.

The email I received reported the results of phase one of a clinical trial conducted by Duke University's pediatric stem cell and cellular therapy program in Durham, North Carolina. Although further research was still being completed, this trial demonstrated the safety of cord blood treatment in autism, and the study showed improvements in behavioural measures. In addition, Duke was overseeing an expanded access program that provided cord blood therapy to children with neurological conditions, including cerebral palsy and autism. The email went on to indicate that if we had our child's cord blood stored with them and had a child with a neurological condition, we could contact Insception for more information.

I was overwhelmed with emotion, excitement, and interest. We had always taken any and every measure available to us to help our son. I called Samir at work immediately, and we discussed this possible new therapy for JSS. The next day, I sent an email to Insception indicating our interest in the program and inquiring as to next steps.

This email began our two-year journey into a novel area we didn't know much about but were willing to explore so we could help our son. Within a week of our inquiry to Insception, we were put in contact with the team at Duke to determine whether JSS would be eligible for their expanded access program. We began our research and numerous inquiries. What were all the possible side effects? How could we get access to the results of the clinical trial, which had been partially completed? Was there a "window of opportunity" with respect to when the stem cells were most effective during a child's development? Could AKS's cord blood be used if JSS's cord blood didn't contain enough stem cells to make the treatment viable? Our list of questions was never-ending. This was an unprecedented treatment; it wasn't even offered in Canada.

There was no way we would put our son in any type of jeopardy, but there was also no way we would let an opportunity like this pass us by if it could help him in his life. We learned that the treatment would consist of a stem cell infusion whereby the patient's cord blood (autologous) or the sibling's cord blood (allogeneic) would be infused into the child through an intravenous therapy line (IV) in the arm. The goal of the treatment was to have the stem cells go into the body through the cord blood infusion and improve neural connectivity in the brain.

On August 20, 2018, we received an email from Duke indicating that they were receiving thousands of inquiries from parents about this new treatment and that it could take up to six months for them to be able to respond. I couldn't even imagine the number of emails Duke was receiving from hopeful parents, just like us, trying to help their children. In my eyes, the dedication and commitment of the team at Duke to help kids with autism was God's work, and we were more than willing to wait our turn in the queue. We are persistent, tenacious, and relentless parents, but we are also patient parents. I would always joke and say I'm like a dog with a bone when it comes to anything important to me in my life. My mantra has always been "I may die trying, but I will never give up."

In the meantime, Duke asked us to fill out a prescreening survey about JSS's medical history and our demographics, as this would help them determine if JSS was eligible for any studies at Duke, including the expanded access program. They also asked us to contact Insception and have the cord blood report, a summary of the quantity and quality of stem cells in a unit of cord blood, sent to them so they could make a preliminary determination about JSS's eligibility for a cord blood infusion. I knew this was going to be a long, intense, and detail-oriented journey, but I was willing to do anything for JSS. In addition to all of my other responsibilities as a mother, a wife, and an autism advocate, I now had another full-time job.

On October 17, 2018, after signing all the relevant consent forms to release confidential information, we breathed a sigh of relief as Inception sent JSS's and AKS's cord blood reports to Duke University. Now, we had to patiently wait for them to review the reports and determine eligibility. I knew we had a long road ahead, but we had completed step one, and that was a step in the right direction. The clinical consultant team at Inception had been instrumental in ensuring that the cord blood reports were sent to Duke as soon as possible. They were always kind and helpful, even when I felt that I had called them perhaps a few too many times. They understood that my calls were coming from a place of love for my son and that my persistence was my dedication to him.

I always say that God and my mom sent angels in our lives when we needed them the most. Some of the conversations I had with the staff at Inception made me feel like I was receiving support directly from my mom. I knew that my mom was doing everything in her power to ensure that her grandson received everything he needed in this earthly realm. This was all welcome divine intervention on our end. We needed all the help we could get.

In between all the stress that we were going through as JSS completed grades 7, 8, and 9, and all the disappointment from the private school rejections, I would regularly check in with Duke every two weeks to find out the status of our application. As I watched JSS struggle with social interactions and deal with behavioural and communication challenges, my mind would turn to the possibility of the treatment at Duke as an avenue through which his life could become a little easier. We wanted to help him, not "cure" him. It was clear in our minds that this treatment wasn't something we were doing to change him—rather, it could give him the opportunity to be everything he wanted to be by unleashing what was already inside him. As his parents, we only wanted to equip him with the best tools so he could live an independent and happy life, grow to his full potential, and fulfill his dreams. If we could decrease his frustration and anxiety and increase his ability to regulate himself, to focus, and positively deal with social situations even a little bit, this was enough for us. If it could allow him to stop taking ADHD medication and melatonin, that would be an added blessing. As I stated before, I knew the ADHD medication was necessary to help him focus and not be overwhelmed, but as a mother who adored her child, every time I gave him the medication, it hurt my heart a little bit.

Once we told JSS about the possibility of the stem cell infusion at Duke, we made sure he understood that we weren't pursuing this as a way to change him. We sat down with him and asked him how he felt about the process and whether he was willing to go ahead with the infusion. We recognized the immense importance of respecting his autonomy as a person, and if we wanted him to be strong and independent, we had to show him that we valued his thoughts and opinions and would respect his decision. We had to be prepared to accept the fact that he might say, "No, I am not doing this."

After explaining the procedure to JSS and the reasons why some people with autism were undergoing this type of procedure, we asked JSS what he thought. His big question was whether it would help him make friends. We explained to him that the infusion may help him with his social communication skills and help him focus better, but there were no guarantees and that this was okay. I explained to him that life is like a puzzle. We all have hundreds and hundreds of pieces that fit into that puzzle during the course of our lives, and that the stem cell infusion at Duke was only one piece of the puzzle, not the entire puzzle. We wanted him to understand that we weren't putting all of our energy and hope into this infusion because we thought it would be a "solution" or "cure" for autism; rather, we wanted him to understand that the infusion was just one piece we were adding to the puzzle of his life in order to help him. Duke was a part of our journey, but not the only part. If the procedure didn't help him with his social communication and focus, that was all right. If anything, our efforts would be a good learning experience. It was very important to me that he understood how this was only one piece of the puzzle of his life that stood alongside all the other therapies, extracurricular activities, social skills groups, and academics he pursued.

JSS listened to everything we had to say, and after asking us one more question about whether it would hurt or not, he told us he wanted to go ahead with the stem cell infusion. The next day, I created a bulletin board for his room. I entitled the bulletin board "My Life," and I drew a puzzle with numerous pieces. I filled in the pieces with the names of places he'd been, people he'd met, schools he'd attended, activities he'd participated in, and the things he'd accomplished in his life. I put Duke down in one piece of the puzzle. I told JSS that some of the pieces were still blank so he could fill them in as he gets older and new opportunities and accomplishments fill his world. I knew that visual representations were important for my son. I wanted him to walk into his room every day and remember all the things that he has accomplished, to know that having autism was a part of him, and that we loved him for who he was and the unique perspective he brought to the world. Whether the treatment helped him or not, we would continue to fill in the blank pieces of the puzzle during the course of his life. That bulletin board still hangs in his room to this day, and we continue to fill in the pieces with words that celebrate his amazing journey.

Life went on, and our inquiries continued. On January 14, 2019, we were informed that they had received the cord blood reports. Although JSS's cord blood unit didn't have the sufficient cell dose for an infusion, AKS's cord blood unit contained a sufficient cell dose, though whether they could be used for the infusion still needed to be determined. However, they still didn't have a time frame or update for when they could proceed with JSS's infusion. Duke was still swamped with applications, and I empathized with them and appreciated how hard they must have been working, so I moved to emailing them every six to eight weeks instead of every two. I didn't want to upset them, but I also didn't want to fall to the back of the line. JSS was getting older, and I thought about all the brain development that occurs during the teenage years. If there was a window of opportunity for the stem cell infusion to be the most effective, I didn't want to miss it.

Finally, on May 14, 2019, I received an email from Duke indicating that although they couldn't proceed with the infusion with JSS's stem cells as there weren't enough, they were ready to determine whether AKS's cells could be used for the infusion. The team at Duke indicated that we would have to complete an HLA (human leukocyte antigen) typing to determine if the siblings were a match.[20] Three out of six HLA markers needed to match in order to use AKS's cord blood unit for JSS. They offered to send us instructions on how to submit AKS's cord blood for analysis if we were interested; however, they informed us that their waitlist was still extremely long, and it would take six to twelve months before they would be able to move forward with the screening process.

I quickly looked up what HLA testing involved and why it was done. I discovered that this type of testing would determine the likelihood of JSS's body accepting AKS's cells rather than rejecting them. Duke also indicated that although AKS had more cells stored than JSS, her numbers were still lower than the average cell dose, and the unit may not be eligible for an infusion by the time they were able to move forward with the screening—that is, as he got older and grew bigger, there was a chance that there wouldn't be enough cells given his increased weight. This was another bump in the road, but we would deal with that in the future. For now, we needed to get the HLA testing done.

I know that the team at Duke was very busy, but I was on a mission, and I persistently sent emails to them about the HLA testing. I must commend the Duke team for being so kind and patient with me. I always appreciate medical teams that understand and empathize with the anguish of desperate parents trying to help their children. The emails from Duke were always respectful and encouraging, and I never felt like I was annoying them. I thank them from the bottom of my heart.

On June 4, 2019, we received information about how to conduct the HLA testing. Without wasting any time, I sent an email the very same day to the appropriate person so we could receive the HLA testing kit from the United States. This test would involve a mouth swab from both kids that we could do at home to determine how many of their HLA markers were a match. It was a substantial cost, and I was thankful to God that we had the ability to pay for these expenses, though my heart ached for those children

---

20   "Human leukocyte antigen (HLA) testing," Canadian Cancer Society, https:// cancer.ca/en/treatments/tests-and-procedures/human-leukocyte-antigen-hla -testing.

who would have liked to have a stem cell infusion done but couldn't afford it. I was grateful, but I also knew that in the future, I wanted to help people access the same opportunities as my son and my family in any way I could.

Gratitude became a way of life for me, and this was thanks to JSS. My soul may have chosen some big challenges in this life, but at least I had the financial means to pay for these expenses. The treatment at Duke was going to cost a lot, and all these tests along the way were also expensive. To this day, I never take anything for granted, and I always try to find ways to help others, whether it's in my daily life or through my advocacy for equality.

On Samir's birthday, we sent the completed HLA tests to a lab in North Carolina to be analyzed. As Samir blew out the candles on his birthday cake and we sang him happy birthday, we both looked at each other and smiled, both of us knowing exactly what he had wished for on his special day.

We tried to be patient as we waited for the results of the HLA testing, but I must confess, I was very stressed out. I must have checked my email a hundred times a day to see if Duke had received and analyzed the results. I tried to alleviate my anguish by praying; praying that regardless of the results, we were giving our son everything he needed in this life to be successful and live his life to the fullest.

On July 16, 2019, Samir's birthday wish came true. The results of the HLA testing came back. All we needed was a three out of six match, but our kids were a perfect match, literally and figuratively. AKS beamed when we told her that she was a perfect match for her brother. Although we still weren't in the clear—AKS's stored cells were still a lower dose than the average cell dose, increasing the possibility of JSS being ineligible for an infusion—we took comfort in the fact that we were one step closer.

Throughout this process, we didn't want AKS to feel left out—as I mentioned before, we were always very conscious of her feelings. It was extremely important for us to reiterate to AKS how important she was to our family and the tremendous supportive role that she played within it. We wanted her to know, without a doubt, that she was equally as important to us as her brother. We told our little six-year-old girl that she was the hero in all of this and that if it wasn't for her, none of this would be happening. She was a gift from God who was giving us emotional support from a very young age, and now, she was coming through for us again during a very nerve-racking but exciting time.

I will never forget the day we told AKS about the results. Both she and her brother were intently listening, and JSS turned to her and said, "Thank you, AKS, for giving me your cells." She turned to him very nonchalantly and said, "You're welcome, Veer ji." She had no idea how incredible this thing that she was doing for her brother was, and she didn't give a second thought to the fact that her cells may not be available to her in the future if she ever needed them. We had of course explained this reality to her, but she had told us it didn't matter because she wanted to help her brother. As her parents, we prayed that she would never need her cells in the future for a medical procedure; as a sister, her only prayer was that the stems cells would help her brother. Her maturity and matter-of-fact attitude brought tears to my eyes and warmth to my soul. She was telling us, "I wouldn't have it any other way; this is my responsibility and dedication to you."

My soul vibrated at a higher frequency. Every day, I was learning the definition of unconditional love over and over, not just by raising a child with autism, but also by watching the love between my beautiful children. My mother had truly sent me an angel on earth, a blessing from God. Thank you, Mom.

The next step would be a screening process whereby Duke would get JSS's medical records from his doctor to determine eligibility for the infusion. From July 2019 to February 2020, I contacted Duke and kept in touch with Insception to determine if there were any changes or updates that would affect us. Throughout this process, I really listened to my heart and soul, and if it told me something or I felt something, I would follow through with it. This was definitely guidance from my angels, and I discovered, through my inquiries, that there was in fact a new format that Duke was using for the cord blood report, which was now called the cord blood unit summary. Insception sent me the new format of the documentation, and on February 21, 2020, I contacted Duke and provided them with AKS's cord blood unit summary in the new format. Keeping up to date on the paperwork and communication was critical.

These experiences taught me to trust my inner voice more and not be afraid to tap into my higher consciousness. If I received a feeling or inclination to do something, I followed it. My view was that as long as I wasn't hurting anyone and I was being kind and respectful in my actions, I would trust my soul more.

On February 25, 2020, I received an email from Duke indicating they were ready to move forward with the screening process. The excitement of this actually happening was filling me with hope and relief. I knew we weren't at the finish line, but every step was a step in the right direction. I immediately emailed Duke back and told them we were ready to proceed. We found out from Duke that twenty to fifty million cells per kilogram of weight was the normal recommendation when it came to an infusion. However, according to their calculation, with JSS's weight and the number of cord blood cells that had been collected from AKS during her delivery, JSS would only receive fifteen million cells per kilogram of weight. In actuality, it would be a little less, as some cells would inevitably be lost during the freezing, thawing, and washing process. We looked into every possibility and made further inquiries with respect to possibly combining JSS and AKS's cells; however, this wasn't possible.

The cost of the infusion was $15,000 US plus expenses. On top of the high cost, there were other risks. This was a new treatment, and there wasn't any concrete data on whether it might be successful, although the preliminary results had looked promising. Additionally, we had always feared that we would miss the "critical window" for JSS to have the infusion due to his weight gain and development, and in this race against time, there were still many other hoops we had to jump through before the infusion actually took place. We needed to make this difficult decision as soon as possible so JSS could receive the maximum number of cells.

Given all this information, it was our decision whether we wanted to proceed. However, Samir and I had been diligently saving to pay for the treatment since the beginning. We happily made sacrifices to provide our son with what he needed—skipping nights out on the town, family vacations, and unnecessary luxuries. We didn't mind doing this at all. We were thankful to even have the means to be able to pay for the treatment. I never stopped thinking about all the people who would be interested in the stem cell infusion and could benefit from the treatment but couldn't afford it.

This further solidified my desire to help people with autism in the future; I just wasn't sure how I was going to do it.

Samir and I decided to proceed with the infusion despite the lower cell count and give JSS the opportunity to receive this promising new therapy. We understood that the infusion may not do anything at all, but we were doing this out of love for our son, and this was enough for us. On February 26, 2020, we sent the consent forms to Duke, giving them access to JSS's medical records, and we took the first major step toward setting the infusion date. JSS also signed the consent forms, an act that was very important to us and him. We wanted him to understand that he was responsible for and had authority over his body and that the infusion would only go ahead if he agreed with it and gave his consent.

By March 4, 2020, we had sent Duke all the required medical documentation. We were told that the medical team would review his file to ensure that he met all of the eligibility criteria. Every day, I would pray; pray that my son had the chance to pursue this therapy so he could live his best life; pray that I was being a good mother to him; pray that I hadn't missed any opportunity that would help him succeed in life; and pray that his angels would always protect and watch over him. In my heart, I knew that I had done everything I could, and now, I would leave the rest in the hands of God and the positive vibrational energy of the universe.

On March 11, 2020, we received the news from Duke we had anxiously been waiting for—JSS passed the medical review, and he was now in the scheduling queue for the infusion. I was so overcome with emotion I immediately broke down in tears. Finally, all of our efforts were going to pay off. We had planted our garden, and now, our flowers were finally going to bloom. However, just as the flowers in a garden can be damaged by severe weather, so too were the fruits of our labour by an unforeseen storm. The world came to a screeching halt with the COVID-19 pandemic at the end of March 2020, and so did our plans to travel to Duke for the infusion. All infusions at Duke had been paused, and JSS's infusion was delayed. He wouldn't lose his spot in the queue, but our concern was that as he gained weight, the number of cells that he would receive per kilogram of weight was also going down. Day after day, week after week, month after month, the reality of this delay caused us heartache, worry, and pain.

The infusions at Duke still weren't happening by the end of May 2020. However, we were still reaching out to Duke regularly and inquiring as to whether we could continue taking any further steps to ensure that when the infusions were reinstated, we could leave immediately. We had to have blood drawn from both kids for blood typing and hemoglobinopathy testing and, additionally, more comprehensive blood work testing for JSS. Our research continued as we tried to understand all the medical terms that arrived in our inbox and the reasons for all of these tests. We wanted to make sure, every step along the way, that we weren't putting JSS in any medical peril.

We also didn't want to forget what our little girl was going through to help her brother. She was prepared to have blood drawn and do anything else for her brother, but as a seven-year-old child, she was also scared. It was a balancing act, and it taught me more patience and perseverance than I had ever learned in my life. I missed my mom and her support and words of encouragement often during this time. I could feel her love and energy in my soul, but sometimes, I just needed her hugs.

But if I needed my mother's hugs, I knew my children needed mine too. At night, I would go into each of my children's rooms and rub their heads and tell them how proud I was of them. I was astounded by AKS's maturity when she would say to me, "Don't stress out, Mommy, everything is going to be okay." I kissed my little *Shakti* goodnight and thanked her again for being in our lives. I loved looking into my children's eyes and seeing their innocence, their unwavering faith, and their passionate belief that everything was going to be okay. It gave me strength.

CHAPTER 13

Help Him, not "Cure" Him

———

"You are never out of time;
You are always just in time."

Mandeep K. Atwal
May 1, 2023

WE STILL DIDN'T HAVE AN INFUSION DATE, BUT BY JULY 2020, Canadians could cross the border to the United States, albeit only by air travel. Duke had also indicated that they anticipated infusions to recommence in mid-July.

But still, challenges kept coming up along the way. The kids were different blood types—did this matter? JSS's blood tests revealed some irregularity in the liver—would this affect the infusion? We received a referral to the gastrointestinal clinic at the Alberta Children's Hospital, as an ultrasound was necessary, another thing we had to deal with before the infusion. We also found out JSS was a carrier of thalassemia, a blood disorder that results in abnormal hemoglobin. What did this mean for the infusion? What did this mean for his life? I was glad we were discovering all these medical issues so they could be dealt with immediately, but I was also scared that all our efforts over the last two years would prove futile.

We spent the summer of 2020 at medical appointments, researching the possible impact of these medical issues on the infusion, communicating with many departments at Duke (including multiple emails determining fee payment), signing numerous consent forms and plans of care, and making arrangements for AKS's care while we were away from home—all without knowing when we were actually going to go. We were constantly worrying about whether we were doing the right thing and whether we were keeping our son safe. I felt like every time we jumped through one hoop, another one was waiting for us. The process felt never-ending.

We really wanted the infusion to take place in the summer because if we went in the fall, JSS could miss up to five weeks of school. At the time, people travelling to Duke University for a treatment from Canada were required to quarantine for two weeks prior to the infusion and then come back to Canada and quarantine for another two weeks. Where would we stay in Duke for three weeks during a pandemic? How would we get food and a rental car? The world had essentially shut down. Taking JSS for the infusion was stressful enough; we didn't need this added stress. We also worried about being away from AKS for three weeks. We didn't have any family who could care for AKS, and although we were so thankful for our heavenly sent angel, Aunty Nancy, who would stay with her and take her to school while we were away, three weeks away would be too long.

The pandemic had turned our five-day trip into a five-week affair. Before the pandemic, we thought we would all travel to Duke together as a family adventure for the four of us. However, taking AKS with us during the pandemic was a nonstarter. Honestly, this was the worst time for the infusion to be scheduled, but we had no choice—time was ticking, and the opportune window for the infusion was closing. We sent a lengthy email to Duke requesting a waiver of the quarantine requirements. Our position was that no one travelling from the US had to abide by these quarantine requirements, despite the fact that the number of infections in almost every state in the US was much higher than ours in Alberta. We provided statistics and the necessary information in the hopes of receiving an exemption from this quarantine period. Samir typed, and I prayed.

After making the required payment for the infusion, on July 17, 2020, we were financially cleared by Duke to receive the infusion. We contacted Insception to give them a heads-up that hopefully, soon, we would be requesting that they send AKS's cells from British Columbia to Duke University. Another layer of complexity was that the medical team who handled the release of the cord blood and all the associated paperwork was located in Mississauga, Ontario, but the cells were stored and shipped from Burnaby, British Columbia—halfway across the country. It was critical that the cells arrive right before the infusion. The last thing we wanted was to travel to Duke for the infusion and be informed that the stem cells had not arrived due to a courier issue. This possible delay due to the COVID-19 pandemic was yet another additional stress. I had no idea how many more steps we had to take and how much more organization this process would entail.

There was a fair amount of documentation we had to complete before the stem cells could even be released and sent to Duke, as this was an area that was strictly regulated by Health Canada. We also learned that before the cells could be sent to Duke, a small segment of the cells had to be sent for testing to a lab in Durham, North Carolina to determine cell viability. If the cells were deemed unviable for an infusion, the entire process would become moot. It was an intricate process that involved multiple organizations and institutions and an additional cost to us.

The cost involved in this entire process never left our minds. We were a single-income family, and we had to make sure we were saving enough money for the treatment and the expenses we would incur during the trip. To say it was an extremely stressful time is an understatement.

Due to the ongoing support, hard work, and diligence of the teams at Duke and Insception, these complex and intricate steps were completed in a timely fashion and all came together at the right time. I saw these organizations as human helpers and healers. I vividly remember a day in September 2020, when I was communicating with the nurse practitioner at Insception whom we had been in contact with over the course of the last two years, and she asked us for a picture of our family for our chart. She indicated that having the faces of the children and their families on the chart was very important to the staff at Insception. This brought tears to my eyes. This was what it was all about. JSS wasn't a number on a file; he was a person with special gifts and talents. We were a *whole* family, passionately trying to help our son. In the middle of an intense storm, it was a wonderful reminder that we and what we were doing as a family mattered. Insception had come into our lives and understood the passionate attempts of parents to do whatever was necessary to give their children the best chance to express their true selves. Thank you, Insception, for reminding us that we mattered.

On September 1, 2020, AKS's test segment was sent by courier to North Carolina, and the waiting game began. This was it. If the cells were viable, the infusion would go ahead, and if they weren't, we would go back to our lives and continue the work we had been doing with our son. Between drop-offs and pickups from school, breakfasts and dinners, homework and extracurricular activities, and frantically stocking up on masks, I would quickly log onto the computer and check if the sample of the stem cells had been received by the lab, whether they had been tested, and if the results had been sent to Duke. I continued sending hopeful emails to the relevant people. It was the only thing on my mind. Autumn was approaching, and as the leaves fell and the world was ravaged by the COVID-19 pandemic, I prayed that we would find our way to Duke and that JSS would reap the benefits of the hard work we had engaged in over the last two years in our pursuit of this treatment.

Thursday, September 24, 2020, was a big day for our family. We received the news that AKS's stem cells were viable for an infusion and that all the medical reviews at Duke were complete. They were ready to book JSS's infusion date. We were further informed that the required two-week quarantine period at Duke had been lifted. This was a huge relief for us, as it meant we would only have to leave AKS for five days; although we would have to quarantine for two weeks once we were back in Canada, we could do it in the comfort of our own home with our daughter.

The infusion was booked for Wednesday, October 21, 2020. We still had to ensure that the rest of the stem cells were sent to Duke from Insception, that our flights and hotel were booked, and that AKS was taken care of while we were gone, but we were elated. Our tenacity was going to pay off. Our son was going to get the opportunity to receive a treatment that may help him express himself in a way that he always longed to—he had a right to be understood, and we were going to do everything we could to ensure that he was. As I held JSS that night and told him the good news, tears streamed down my face, and my mind took me back to the first time I held my little boy in my arms when he was born. I remember vowing to him that I would be the best mother I could for him and that I would give him every opportunity to be happy, fulfill his dreams, and be confident and courageous. Every action I had taken as his mother during his life, I had taken with love and dedication. We had not even gone for the treatment yet, but I felt we had accomplished something monumental.

That very same day, we booked our flights and hotel to Raleigh, North Carolina. Duke University is located in Durham, North Carolina, which is about a thirty-minute drive from Raleigh. The pandemic was at its height, and there was only one flight available to Raleigh through Dallas, Texas. There was no margin for error. If we missed our flight or didn't catch our connecting flight, the infusion wouldn't happen. I had faith that our angels and the positive universal energy was on our side. I always told my kids that if you have faith, believe in good, and put positive energy into the universe, it will always come back to you tenfold. I also knew that we had some amazing angels in heaven casting a protective net over us who would ensure that everything worked out for us. As I mentioned before, whenever you do something out of love, there is a positive vibrational force that emerges and aids you. We can all experience this positivity if we believe in it and if our actions are sincere. Any anxiety I felt as we approached the date of the infusion was neutralized by a calming vibrational power that surrounded me. I knew that this calming, warm, and comforting energy was my mom showing me that although she was no longer in the physical world, her love and dedication to me extended beyond the earthly realm.

We spent the month of October in frantic preparation. Between our daily struggles, we had phone calls with Insception and Duke involving final reviews of JSS's medical history, signing consents, confirming schedules, and getting specific details about the infusion and hospital protocols. We also arranged to receive and then teach JSS all the schoolwork he would miss during the five days we would be at Duke. It was a scary time to travel due to the COVID-19 pandemic, as no one fully understood the virus; nonessential travel was prohibited, border agents could refuse entry into the United States, and vaccines weren't yet available to us. We had to make sure we had all of our bases covered, including getting a letter from Duke explaining why we were crossing the border and seeking this treatment for our son.

Our stress further intensified when five days before the infusion, the stem cells had been held up somewhere in Cincinnati, Ohio. With the infusion only five days away, the ongoing delays due to the pandemic, and a weekend falling in between, I was in a panic. But miraculously, the stem cells arrived on the very day they were supposed to; somehow, they made their way from Cincinnati, Ohio to Durham, North Carolina, in just a couple of hours. Things continued to fall into place.

During all our chaotic running around and packing, we never forgot about AKS and her feelings. We reminded our little girl that she was the hero in the events that were unfolding. She was very brave to stay at home without us during such an uncertain time. As we all know, the COVID-19 pandemic caused such turmoil in the world down to the everyday lives of so many people, especially children. Children needed extra support as they returned to school after being home and isolating for six months, and still our brave little eight-year-old girl was ready to let her entire family leave the country, not knowing what circumstances we might encounter travelling during such a difficult time.

The words of my dear friend, Margaret Davenport-Freed, echoed in my mind. She had explained to me that I was the main cog in our family wheel, and the role I played as a mother made the wheel turn smoothly. I really liked this analogy, and I extrapolated it even further. Every member of our family is a cog in our family wheel. If each member of the family does their part, the wheel will move smoothly; however, if even one member doesn't do their part, the wheel stops turning smoothly. This doesn't mean we can't stop along the journey of life for repairs, but once everything is back on track, we all have to do our part. The wheel doesn't have to move quickly; it just has to keep moving forward. We wanted AKS to know that our family was gaining strength and feeling empowered because she was doing her part with a grace and maturity beyond her years. She was a very powerful cog in our family wheel.

The night before we left, I led JSS to the puzzle board in his room and reminded him again that going to Duke was only a piece of his life's puzzle and that it didn't in any way encompass the entire puzzle. I wanted to reinforce that we were going to Duke to help him, not "cure" him. I then packed last-minute items, including food, as we didn't know what would be available to us due to COVID-19 and all of the lockdowns. It's a good thing I did—as it would turn out, finding places to eat close to our hotel was another challenge we faced during our trip.

As I closed up our one suitcase and three backpacks, I said a heartfelt prayer to God and my mom. I felt nervous, excited, overwhelmed, scared, and happy all in the same moment. I had been running around at the speed of light for the last month trying to get everything in order. I was exhausted, but I reminded myself that my physical strength was directly determined by my mental strength. I had to find strength in the love that was carrying us to Duke. I had to reach deep inside myself and find that last push of energy and resilience so I could help my son and give him the support that he needed at this time. He was the one that was going through the physical treatment, not me.

I will never forget the morning of Monday, October 19, 2020. We said our tearful goodbyes to AKS, thanked Aunty Nancy for being there for us when we needed her the most, and headed to the airport. When we arrived, it was an eerie feeling; only the three of us were passing through security at the international terminal. Usually, people are shoulder to shoulder, the lineups are huge, and there's a lot of hustle and bustle. Instead, that day, it felt like a scene from a movie where the world had come to an end and we were the only three people left standing.

We boarded the plane and headed to Dallas, Texas, where we would catch the connecting flight to Raleigh, North Carolina. We were delayed by one hour heading into Dallas, and Samir and I were exchanging nervous glances at each other during the flight. There were no other flights to Raleigh that day. It was essential for us to arrive at Duke that same night, as JSS had an appointment for some final tests at 8 a.m. the next morning, the day before the infusion. As I sat in my seat, praying and keeping my faith that everything would work out, the pilot announced that somehow, we were getting an incredible tailwind, and we would in fact make it to Dallas on time. In the physical world, this was described as an incredible tailwind, but I knew that in the spiritual world, it was our angels adding some extra angel wings to the wings of the plane. We had earth angels waiting for us at Duke University, and we had heavenly angels who were helping us along our way. My heart and soul were resonating a peaceful energy; a spiritual power was sending me comfort and reassurance that everything was going to work out, and that the infusion was going to be a success.

Our travel day ended with us arriving at our hotel at 11:30 p.m. on Monday night, and as JSS laid his head on his pillow, we breathed a sigh of relief. I looked at my son sleeping and softly kissed his cheek, promising him I would spend my entire life ensuring he and his sister had everything they needed. This wasn't just my responsibility; it was my honour and my soul journey.

When we got up the next day, I decided not to give JSS his ADHD medication. My intuition was telling me that since he was getting his final testing done on Tuesday and his infusion on Wednesday, I didn't want any other medication in his body that might inhibit the work of the stem cells. This wasn't a medical recommendation, more of a mother's gut feeling. JSS and I met with the team at Duke at 8 a.m. that morning. Due to the COVID-19 pandemic, only one parent was allowed into the hospital. It was wonderful to finally see the faces of the team that had been supporting us through this process over the last two years. The team at Duke continued to interact with us in a caring and supportive manner as JSS completed some final blood work, a physical checkup, and a review of his medical history.

It was a different world at Duke due to the COVID-19 pandemic. We had to wear masks everywhere, including outside of the hospital, even if it was just the three of us walking alone. With strict lockdown measures in place, the ability to just grab food from the hospital was nonexistent. It was probably one of the worst times to travel, let alone go to another country for a medical procedure. I stayed in the hotel with JSS and gave him the food I brought along as Samir would comb the streets looking for something we could eat. We also had to be very careful what we gave JSS due to his tree nut and peanut allergy. The last thing we needed was for him to have an anaphylactic reaction the day before the infusion. It's amazing how much strength you can find within yourself when you're passionately pursuing something that you know is important to your soul. Samir and I were functioning on limited sleep, limited food, and tremendous anxiety, yet we still had more energy than I ever thought we could in this type of circumstance. Some may call it adrenaline; I called it soul strength.

The day had finally arrived—Wednesday, October 21, 2020. As JSS got ready for the infusion, I reassured him that he was going to get through this treatment with the same strength and resilience he had when he conquered all the other challenges in his life. Once again, only one parent was allowed in during the infusion due to COVID-19, so Samir was on a Zoom call with us through the entire procedure. The nurses and doctors had indicated that the only possible problem JSS could face was an allergic reaction to remnants of the preservative that was used while freezing and storing the stem cells. If that occurred, the infusion would have to be paused in order to give JSS medication to control the allergic reaction. If the reaction was too severe, the infusion would have to be stopped.

The doctors started an IV drip and gave JSS anti-allergy medication, which was standard practice before the infusion. Around 11:00 a.m., a little bag of red stem cells was brought into the room. I looked at it and thought to myself that two years of research, dedication, perseverance, and hope was in that little bag of AKS's stem cells. As I looked at the stem cells, I thanked AKS on behalf of our family for this opportunity, and I asked God to bless her and keep her safe. Our little angel was probably busy at school, playing, learning, and chatting with her friends, not realizing the true impact of the gift she had given her brother.

As the cells entered JSS's body, I prayed.

I prayed on my grandfather's rosary, the rosary that had been in JSS's room since before his birth. I thanked God for letting us see this day, and I asked Him to protect our son and keep him under His loving care. Although JSS did end up having a mild allergic reaction during the infusion, this complication was anticipated. The infusion was paused to give him additional allergy medication, and he was able to continue and complete the infusion.

As I saw the last of the stem cells enter his body through the IV, I said to JSS with tear-filled eyes, "You did it; we did it!" I looked over at Samir and smiled. We didn't need to say anything. I saw the joyful tears in his eyes, and I could understand every emotion he was feeling—we were communicating our feelings through our souls. This was a huge day for our family and our soul journey. It didn't matter now whether the treatment worked or not; what mattered was that we had done everything in our power to help our son show the world his true self. Autism is, and will always be, a part of the beautiful person he is, and we would not have it any other way.

◆ ◆ ◆

We are often asked if the treatment worked for JSS. Medical professionals and friends have told us they see a big change in him. He is calmer, more focused, and more socially aware. He has better social communication and reasoning skills. He is able to better regulate himself, and he asks less repetitive questions, allowing for more natural conversations with people. We as parents have also witnessed these big positive changes in JSS since the infusion. A big victory for me personally is that he no longer needs his ADHD medication or melatonin.

Was the infusion worth it? My answer would be that even if we didn't see these big positive changes and improvements, it was worth it because anything done out of soul love is, in and of itself, a victory—a noble victory.

CHAPTER 14

The Missing Peace

———

IN 2022, SAMIR AND I CELEBRATED OUR TWENTIETH WEDDING anniversary, JSS turned sixteen, and AKS turned ten. Amid those milestones, the tenth year of my mom's departure from the physical world passed as well. I'm thankful that my mom continues to send me messages from the heavenly realm. I could write a whole other book about how my spiritual understanding has completely opened up and grown deeper due to my experiences, but that's for another time. All I know is that I have never been without her, and I have never been alone. This reassurance gave me comfort every day and helped ease my heartache on those very difficult days. I also remembered her advice to stop and smell the roses; I do this every day.

It took me over a year to write this book. A paragraph here, a paragraph there, while sitting in coffee shops or in my car, waiting for the kids after school, at birthday parties, at their extracurricular activities. I would try and find the time to write whenever I could to passionately put on paper all the things we've gone through so I could help and encourage others to persevere during their most difficult times. Our family's experiences have helped our souls' strength to grow and radiate. We all have God-given strength and power in our soul, but it's our job to find a way to tap into this strength and use it to make our life circumstances better. This isn't always easy, and it can take a lifetime to develop. I'm still working on it and will continue to do so for the rest of my life. However, at this point in my life, I feel strong enough to share our story to help other families tap into their strength. I want other families to know that they aren't alone in their struggles and that they too can draw upon their inner strength to persevere through their challenges.

Writing this book has been one of the most rewarding experiences of my life. It has helped me heal, and it has helped me grow as I put down on paper all the things that I have gone through as a mother, a daughter, and a wife. I always thought I would write this book when JSS was much older and I had helped him in every way I could. I thought at that time there would be some finality in our autism journey, but I realized no such thing exists. This journey is ongoing, and not just because my son has autism, but because he is my son and I am his mother. Everything is not going to suddenly be perfect one day; it's not perfect for anyone, but if we're learning, growing, loving, helping, and moving forward, we have created our perfect journey. When I came to this realization, I sat down and typed the first words of my book.

It seems like just yesterday we started our autism journey as we nervously sat in various doctors' offices listening to what challenges JSS would face in his life. We were ready to pursue any and every avenue we could in order to give him the best chance in life to express his true self and accomplish his dreams. However, when I look at my son and see this handsome young man standing before me, I realize that we didn't meet with these doctors just yesterday; instead, it has taken sixteen years of love, dedication, tears, acceptance, and growth to get to this day.

We faced some very hard times and often felt very demoralized and scared, but we had to remind ourselves that on May 12, 2006, we were given a very precious and delicate gift from God. It was our souls that would give us the direction and answers we needed to give our son everything he required to be successful and strong in this sometimes not-so-kind world. Would I change our journey? No, it made me who I am today, and it gave me some very important gifts—increased knowledge about autism, greater empathy, and passionate advocacy. Understanding how a child with autism like my son navigates a world that doesn't always have space for him or understand him is a gift I'm blessed to receive. It has given me a more compassionate outlook on life and has taught me a level of patience my soul needed to learn. I have developed a deep-rooted appreciation for those living with autism and other special needs. I may not fully understand the challenges that a person living with autism or other diagnosed conditions faces on a daily basis, but I do empathize with them, gain strength from them, and recognize how brave they are to face an often judgmental world.

Finally, the gift of passionate advocacy has become my soul journey. Whether it's writing this book, conducting autism presentations, meeting other mothers and sharing our feelings or swapping information on available funding and supports, creating awareness groups, or talking to people in my community who others may just walk past, I can unequivocally say that my soul has found its purpose. I want individuals living with autism and other special needs in my community, in my country, and in the world to know they are seen, they are heard, they are respected, and they are important. This has become a natural and daily part of my life. Through this type of leadership, one is given the opportunity to serve humankind.

The last few years have been an even greater time of growth and understanding for me due to the COVID-19 pandemic. As everything was shutting down and we felt more isolated from the world, I started to gain real-life insight into how those living with autism must feel on a daily basis. Isolation, loneliness, fear of losing our routines, and not understanding what was going to happen in the world when we stepped outside of our doors were things that people on the spectrum must feel regularly. I also developed an even deeper sensitivity, empathy, and compassion for those who deal with this reality for a lifetime and not just a few years.

As I watched schools close down and online learning begin, I thought of all those children with autism who lost their daily educational assistants and supports at school. Their routines had just been eliminated in a matter of days. JSS was lucky that I was at home with my kids and that I could spend six hours a day in his room, helping him stay focused and to keep up with the pace of online learning and all the social communication that came along with it. Expressive and receptive language was already a challenge for him in the classroom where there was face-to-face instruction, but to understand all the instructions, social nuances, and quick communication of his classmates while looking at a computer screen was definitely an overwhelming challenge.

COVID-19 further exacerbated all the social challenges that children on the spectrum deal with on a daily basis. It was hard for a child on the spectrum to just pick up the phone and call a friend during the COVID-19 pandemic when their friendships didn't extend beyond the walls of the classroom. This time in my life further reinforced the true difference between acceptance and inclusion. Acceptance may involve talking to a child with autism in the classroom, but true inclusion involves making them a part of your life outside of the classroom.

Moreover, my mind turned to all of the kids whose parents had to work full-time, those children living in poverty, and the parents of children on the spectrum who spoke English as a second language. What was going to happen to them? There was a lot of discussion about the effects of COVID-19 on "neurotypical" children, who lost sports teams, clubs, and extracurricular activities. All of these losses are very important to rectify; however, the loss of an already minimal support system for those living with autism wasn't a top priority in the community. Agencies that typically helped people with special needs were doing their best, but we needed a greater community response to deal with all the setbacks children with special needs were facing. We need to value those kids with special needs as much as we value the loss of a support system for "neurotypical" children. One should not be valued at the exclusion of the other. All children are important, and not all children require the same level or type of support. I say this as a mother of both a "neurotypical" child and of a child on the spectrum. We have a community responsibility to support every child. We can't make a difference in the future if we don't set a positive precedent today.

COVID-19 started on the other side of the earth, but before we knew it, it was knocking on our door. We are all interconnected within a global community, and we have more similarities than differences. The actions of one person on the other side of the world can affect us in ways we can't even begin to understand or imagine. I believe the same rings true in my advocacy work for autism. In our everyday lives, this may be hard to see, but the COVID-19 pandemic opened my eyes in many ways. During the pandemic, we all wanted to be safe, to ensure that our basic needs were met, and to be around the people we loved. I realized that this journey that we're all taking at the same time, but in different circumstances, is similar in many respects. We all want happiness, security, peace, and love.

I also realized there wasn't any amount of money that could immediately eliminate a virus that had essentially taken over the world.

I learned that although I might not be able to single-handedly change the world and create an inclusive and equitable environment for every individual living with autism, I can make positive changes in my community every day that can radiate and eventually reach corners of the earth that I have never even seen—just like the COVID-19 pandemic. Small, positive, and kind gestures that don't seem like much can create a ripple effect that can change the world. Don't doubt your strength as a human being to make a difference. When we improve the quality of our community, we are in fact improving the quality of our world. True acceptance and inclusion can only occur once we come together as a community, a society, a country, and a human race and realize we're all more alike than we are different. By embracing our global and spiritual responsibilities, we ensure the betterment of humanity and raise the world's spiritual vibration.

Some people may call me an idealist and claim that all the things I'm saying are just powerless words, but I challenge you to try. Every small step I've taken in my life has brought me to where I am today. I encourage you to take that small positive first step, whether it's in your home or in your community. My first small positive step was the day I took my son to his first speech therapy session. Some may have thought, "You worry too much; just let him be and he will be fine," or "Why are you trying to get him to speak? He has his lot in life, let him live it." Did I lose anything by taking him to speech therapy and pushing him to tap inside of himself and find his strength? No, I didn't—and in fact, I gained not only his voice, but also my soul's purpose.

We create our lot in life. When I finally accepted my life circumstances and realized what my soul journey entailed, I felt like I had found the missing piece in my life. When you find the missing piece, you find the peace you've been missing. By doing what you're meant to do on this earth, true peace, true joy, and true soul elevation is yours. Your soul knows your destiny. Take the time to ask. Take that first step.

I have met people who think that those with autism or other special needs are somehow weak and that Samir and I must resign ourselves to "take care of" or "serve" a child with special needs for the rest of our lives.

However, we believe the complete opposite; we believe that our son is the very definition of strength and that his unique view of the world is leading us on a path of greater understanding and spiritual growth. Autism has given my son the special ability to bring an innocence, open-mindedness, and unique perspective to a world that can be very closed-minded and judgmental. This is a very powerful spiritual gift that demonstrates great strength, not weakness. The only reason those living with autism may be vulnerable is because of those who take advantage of their innocence and open-mindedness.

Individuals living with autism face tremendous obstacles, and they teach us very important lessons about resilience, courage, strength, patience, understanding, compassion, and love. Although these beautiful qualities are often lacking in our world, these are the qualities we are all sent to earth to learn. I am so happy that I have chosen a soul journey that warrants standing up for justice, equality, and inclusion. I have learned that if you don't stand for something, you can't achieve anything. I have my son to thank for this life lesson.

◆ ◆ ◆

A few weeks ago, JSS said to me that he wanted to spend more time with me and create more memories with me, as he knows I'm not going to be here forever. I reassured him that I still have a lot to do on this earth before I go, but the thing that brought the biggest smile to my face, and the most peace in my heart, was him explaining all the things he wanted to accomplish in his life. He confidently told me that after high school, he wants a career in coding or digital technology, that he will get a good job, that he will get married, and that one day, he'll have children of his own. As a mother, I still worry about the small things, like when he heads out for walks or bike rides on his own, when he goes to his part-time job, or when he talks about driving in the city, but I have to trust that all the years we spent teaching him how to live in this world while still being himself will carry him as he discovers more of his talents and meets new people. Although I may worry, I have no doubt that all his dreams of having a successful career and family life will come true.

I know I can't trust the entire world, but I must trust the loving upbringing we've given him and the confidence that he has in himself. I would often say to my family and friends that when JSS finishes school, has a job, gets married, has kids, and does everything he wants to, then I'll breathe. I've learned now that I need to breathe every day because every day is an accomplishment; every day is a victory. I can't hold my breath for that one big day. Today is that one big day. I don't hold my breath anymore. I breathe every day.

I take great pride that our family hasn't grown and developed in a "typical" way. JSS has taught us about true "diversity." I have learned that to compare yourself to others in order to judge your own success is, in and of itself, a failure, but to persevere and blossom at your own pace, and in your own unique way, is true success. Regardless of how old JSS is, it will never be easy for us to watch him struggle or face hardships, but I've realized the best thing I can do for him is give him strength, self-confidence, and the space to grow as an independent person who is valued and loved. We also remind him to never let a diagnosis define him or to submit to standards and expectations that move him away from expressing his true self. We live in faith, not fear.

Every day that we face a challenge, celebrate a success, or advocate for autism, we put one drop in a bucket. At the end of the day, one drop doesn't seem like much, but by the end of the week, the end of the month, the end of the year, twenty years later, or even fifty years later, those drops will fill and overflow that bucket. At that time, I'll feel I've won a noble victory knowing that my son has, and hopefully others have, a bucket full of strength.

I want to end this book with a special poem for my children. Please take care of yourself and others, stay strong, and believe in your soul journey.

Our Noble Victory

*"As my soul leaves this earthly dimension
and heads to a spiritual realm,
Please know that I love and adore you, my precious children.*

*I will never be far from your heart,
though I may be far from sight;
Look beyond the physical truths of earth
and see the power in the light.*

*Never give up on your dreams or doubt who you are;
The definition of who you are should never be found from afar.*

*Look within your soul and trust this guiding force.
It will ensure that you are never off course.*

*Live with integrity, love, and care,
Help make every circumstance in life fair.*

*Fight against injustice, and others you should lift;
Compassion and empathy truly are a gift.*

*Never give up your principles or submit to something wrong.
Your soul is the guide, and you must follow along.*

*Although the time has come for us to part ways,
The soul lessons that you taught me will never go away.*

*I carry your love in the essence of myself;
Until we meet again, honour your true self."*

Mandeep K. Atwal
July 25, 2022

Acknowledgements

———

I AM THANKFUL FOR THE CHALLENGES I HAVE HAD TO FACE IN this lifetime because I know they have been stepping stones for me to reach a higher level of soul growth. I believe the soul can only grow by facing challenges and by helping others heal.

I want to start by thanking God, my mom, my maternal grandfather (Papa ji), and my guardian angels in heaven who continued to show me the signs I needed to see in order to complete this book.

Mom, my heart still aches for you, but my soul knows you never left me. Although your physical presence is no longer with me, you have shown me that love transcends the physical realm and that there isn't any amount of distance that can take you away from the essence of my soul. I used to think that if I ever lost you, my life would be over, and I wouldn't be able to go on. However, ironically, losing you made me stronger, made my soul more balanced, and made me a better mother and person. You were ready to move mountains for me, and so am I ready to move mountains for my children. Thank you for teaching me what a mother's love truly encompasses. I love you and I miss you with every single breath. Until we meet again—thank you for being my mom, my best friend, and my number one fan. I hope in every lifetime you are my mom and I am your daughter.

Papa ji, we lost you when I was only fourteen years old. I didn't realize until I was in my forties that you have always been present in my life. Thank you for being the heavenly powerhouse that you are. Although we didn't get a lot of time together on earth, I hope I've made you proud. I treasure the notes and letters you wrote to me when I was a child. I miss you, I love you, and I respect you. Thank you from the depths of my soul for all of your guidance.

I want to thank my dear son, JSS. If you could see my soul, you would be able to understand the immense love and respect that I have for you. You have taught me the true meaning of unconditional love. You are the reason I sat down and wrote this book, and I thank you from the bottom of my heart for teaching me about autism so I could help others. I had no idea when I held you for the first time how much knowledge, strength, and determination you would bring into our lives. You have grown into such a strong, compassionate, intelligent, brave, and handsome young man. You have faced every challenge in your life with a resilience that astounds me. You truly exemplify the meaning of your name—"Guardian of Victory." You are my child, but in so many ways, you are my mentor and my soul teacher. You are teaching me how to live my best life and helping my soul to grow. I know that you can accomplish anything you put your mind to. Always remember that no matter what storm life may throw at you, your mom, dad, and baby sister will be standing beside you to guide you, help you, or just hold your hand. We have been blessed to be able to share this life journey with you. We love you and respect you more than you will ever know. May God bless you with everything you need.

My precious daughter, AKS; my firecracker and, in many ways, my mini mother. You were born nine months after my mom passed away—a gift from God and my mom. You gave me faith and hope at a very difficult and desperate time in my life. You were the light at the end of the tunnel and the hand that reached down from heaven and grabbed me as I was falling. You brought a piece of heaven to earth with you the day you were born. It has been a blessing from God to watch you grow. You have supported your brother and parents in ways your little soul doesn't even realize. True to the meaning of your name—"Noble Woman"—you're always choosing the noble path and standing up for those who need a little extra love and help in this world. I have tremendous reverence and admiration for your strength, confidence, intelligence, and compassion for those living with autism. You have a brilliant and dynamic aura, and every day, you make a positive difference in this world. JSS is blessed to have a sister like you!

When I think of you, my heart and soul are filled with so much love, pride, and respect. We love you and we absolutely adore you.

To my soul partner, Samir. People will search a lifetime for someone who will accept them for who they are, someone who will support them in their soul growth. I am lucky enough to have found that connection and bond with you. We seem to come together so naturally. Our similar passion for standing up against injustice definitely brings us closer. You give me the freedom and space to grow as a person, but whenever I need you, I know you'll be right there. You are a dedicated father to our children and a supportive husband. We succeed in raising JSS and AKS because we're both prepared to always put the children first. Setting aside our own needs is not always easy, but the fact that we are always on the same page with respect to doing what is best for them has made my love for you grow more intense over the years. We have the same silly sense of humour, and this has definitely made me smile on those very tough days. Our journey has taught me that the foundation of a marriage lies in respect for one another. Respect nurtures love, respect ensures soul growth, and respect creates a strong and unbreakable family bond. Although life has thrown many challenges our way, we have created a beautiful and unified family. Thank you for always supporting me. I love you, and I respect you.

Thank you to my many soul sisters whose constant love, support, and encouragement has carried me through my darkest days. I knew the first time I met all of you that we had a soul connection. The manner in which all of you support JSS means the world to me, and the fact that you all loved and accepted him for who he is brought me even closer to you. Thank you.

Susie Thind, you have been a constant source of support in my life. You have given me strength when I was the most vulnerable, and I know I can count on you every day. I know it would take me lifetimes to repay you for everything that you have done for me. I will never forget those sad days when Mom had passed away and I had a newborn in my arms. Anytime I would pick up the phone to reach out to you, you were always there to support me. You taught me to be more open to the world and to trust the people who crossed my path. Your soul is filled with such purity and innocence, and I am blessed to call you my soul sister. I love you from the depths of my soul.

Maira Hassan, you have always amazed me with your strength and how much you do for others. I consider you my soul teacher. I have always looked up to you as an older sister—even though I'm older than you! Your composure and sense of calm in tough situations is a quality I really admire, and I aspire to be like you in so many ways. You have not only carried me, but also my family through so many situations. To me, you signify a very powerful energy that has a peaceful effect on me. You were with me in the delivery room when JSS was born, and as you know, that was the beginning of a new and challenging journey for me. I know that God brought you into my life as a guiding force as I navigate my soul journey. Thank you for never letting me down. I love you, and even though you show your love in the things that you do for others, I will continue to force you to say the words "I love you!"

Rav Lotey-Chana, your passion for life and compassion for others is what struck me when I met you. You are a giver, and you don't expect anything in return. In this world, people like you are hard to come by. I wasn't surprised at all when you told me you were a nurse at the children's hospital. You taught me to take care of myself, and you always lift me up. The fact that JSS is so naturally drawn to you speaks volumes about the power of your soul. Thank you for always encouraging me, telling me how proud you are of our family, and for teaching me to live! I love you so very much.

Eileen Marikar, although we met later in life, we always said it felt like we've known each other forever. I will never forget the first time your eyes filled up with tears when I was telling you about some of our hardships. You took the time to learn about autism, and you always listened so attentively when I told you about our many challenges and experiences. This demonstrated to me the compassion in your soul and how you feel with your heart. Your children also welcomed and included JSS, and this meant so much to us, as we had many experiences where we were excluded. It's easy for people to say they accept everyone, but it's quite another to actually include someone. Thank you for giving me hope that there are amazing people in the world like you who say what they mean and do what they say. I really love you and respect you.

Janice Ferguson, when we reconnected after not seeing each other for twenty-five years, it was like I had known you for many lifetimes. You were right when you said we have a "soulful friendship." Your spirituality and faith in mankind was so refreshing and made my soul feel a peace that comes after a storm. Your sincerity, optimism, and beautiful smile always gave me the energy and strength that I needed to sit down and put into words what I was feeling in my heart. I love you, your energy, and your soul. Thank you for always keeping me on track with what I am supposed to do in this world.

Anna Spadafora Kalika, your words "you got this" resonate in my head when I feel overwhelmed and I wonder how I'm going to complete all the things on my to-do list. Your positivity and faith in God is what brought us together and what keeps our friendship strong. Thank you for always accepting JSS for who he is and for always reminding me that what I do for my son is not just "enough," but above and beyond. Autism mothers need to hear that every once in a while. Love you, sister.

Thank you to the wonderful school moms that I met when AKS started at WS School. You all showed a genuine concern about JSS and the struggles I was facing. Thank you for taking the time to ask questions and learn more about autism. You are a caring, loving, and supportive group of ladies. You stood without judgment, and I am honoured to call you my school tribe. I love you all.

Thank you to all our family and friends who have watched our journey from the start and encouraged us to keep going and beamed with pride as JSS succeeded. Your support gave us the strength and determination to keep moving forward.

Thank you to my uncle Rajinder Singh Gill (Mama ji) and my aunt Surinder Kaur Sekhon (Mami ji). I knew I could always count on you, and this gave me so much comfort. Not only did you provide us with emotional support, but all the food and treats you dropped off for us made a world of difference on those days I was running on empty. Mami ji, thank you for always treating me like your daughter, and for all your blessings and prayers. I will never forget everything you've done for us. I love you both so very much.

Thank you to the Bhogal Family and Upinder Kaur Bhogal (Massi ji) for all of your love and support. Massi ji, you were my mom's best friend and soul sister, and you have always held such a special place in my heart. After losing my mother, I longed for a mother figure who would hold me up on those tough days. Thank you for standing by me as a mother when I needed my mother the most. I have so much love and respect for you. God bless you.

Thank you to my brother, Hardeep Bhogal, for all the hours you spent helping me create the vision for my book's front and back cover pages. Your hard work and attention to detail made the process that much easier for me. You helped me create a perfect reflection of what was in my heart. Thank you and God bless you.

Nancy Fishman, aka Aunty Nancy, you came to me when I was juggling life with two kids and grieving the loss of my mother. I immediately felt comfortable with you, and I always felt like my mom was visiting me when you came over to care for the children. You treated my children like your own grandchildren. You gave me the time to regroup and come back refreshed as a stronger and calmer mother. The fact that I had purchased a gift for you when I was with my mom, years before I even met you, confirmed in my mind that you are an angel sent to us from my mom. You are our family. We love you, and we cherish your presence in our lives.

Thank you to Margaret Davenport-Freed for being the catalyst for the fire in me to sit down and write this book. Thank you for connecting me to my soul and to my loved ones who watch me from heaven. Your encouragement and love allowed me to publish this book and help other people, just as you have done for your entire life. Thank you for all your guidance and support. I love you. God bless you.

I would like to extend a big thank you to all the angels who appeared during the course of our journey—all the teachers, educational assistants, and therapists who gave JSS extra support, the ones who would send me messages just to let me know everything was going okay, and those who sincerely listened to me as I explained to them, with tear-filled eyes, how much JSS means to us and how we would do anything and everything to help him.

Thank you to JSS's first ever educational assistants, Amy Davies and Margaret Pickering. Your love for JSS and genuine desire to help him succeed filled my soul with hope. You both were a godsend, and your commitment to children with special needs taught me how to be a better mother. Your loving actions, compassionate understanding, and sincere empathy embraced me and held me up on some very tough days. God sent you as angels in our lives, and your presence is a blessing. We love you both very much.

Thank you Jessica Hughes and Stephanie Warkentin for supporting not just JSS, but me personally as a friend as I dealt with my mom's sickness and passing, and then helping me when I was bedridden during my pregnancy with AKS. You came into our home as aides and left as friends. I hope you both know that although many years have passed, we will never forget what you did for JSS and our family. We love you.

We extend our sincere gratitude to all the medical professionals who helped us and gave us the support and guidance we needed to do what was best for our son. I would like to extend a heartfelt thank you to Dr. Tracy Taylor and Barbara Patterson. Trust in any relationship is important, but when you entrust the well-being of your child—your heart and soul—into someone else's hands, you pray you're making the right decision. I can unequivocally say that no other medical professionals could have taken care of JSS and our family the way both of you have. Often, medical professionals are told not to get emotionally attached, but I feel proper care can't be given unless there is emotional involvement. You both exemplify remarkable human beings because you also involve your heart in your medical treatment. You both looked at us through a compassionate lens along with a medical lens, and this combination is hard, if not impossible, to find. Thank you from the bottom of our hearts for your medical care and your compassionate hearts. We have so much love and respect for you both.

Thank you to Rochelle Hughes, our caseworker for over a decade at Family Support for Children with Disabilities. You met us very early in our journey and your kindness, support, guidance, and understanding made the process so much easier for us. Your genuine concern for children with special needs was evident in how hard you worked to ensure that our son received the supports that he required. Thank you for being a part of our journey, and for rejoicing with us as we shared JSS's accomplishments and achievements.

Thank you to the people I met in the autism community who said the right thing when I needed to hear it the most. I am honoured to be a part of this wonderful community. I look forward to working with you in the future so we can continue our advocacy for autism.

Thank you to the people I met in my day-to-day life that didn't judge me and instead offered a helping hand. Your compassion and empathy didn't go unnoticed, and I pray that when you need a helping hand, an angel is sent your way.

Last but certainly not least, thank you to the amazing staff at FriesenPress for your support, guidance, and words of encouragement as I was navigating my publishing journey. It is because of you that my book is out in the world, and in the hands of those who need it. Thank you for helping me to launch my platform so I may fulfill my soul journey, and continue to passionately advocate for autism.

I consider it a blessing to have all of these amazing and unique souls in my life who have been pillars of strength during some very trying times, who have helped me face my challenges head-on, and who have helped my soul to grow. As the saying goes, it takes a village to raise a child; it also takes a village to support the parents and guardians of individuals who are on the autism spectrum. There is no noble victory that comes without its challenges, and my family has definitely faced its fair share. I am thankful for all the loved ones in our lives who held us up.

Printed in the USA
CPSIA information can be obtained
at www.ICGtesting.com
LVHW090903271023
761853LV00031B/104/J